The Great Spring

ALSO BY NATALIE GOLDBERG

MEMOIR

Long Quiet Highway: Waking Up in America
The Great Failure: My Unexpected Path to Truth
Living Color: Painting, Writing, and the Bones of Seeing

POETRY

Chicken and in Love
Top of My Lungs: Poems and Paintings

WRITING BOOKS

Writing Down the Bones: Freeing the Writer Within
Wild Mind: Living the Writer's Life
Thunder and Lightning: Cracking Open the Writer's Craft
Old Friend from Far Away: The Practice of Writing Memoir
The True Secret of Writing: Connecting Life with Language

NOVEL

Banana Rose: A Novel

NOTEBOOK

Essential Writer's Notebook

DOCUMENTARY FILM

Tangled Up in Bob: Searching for Bob Dylan
(with filmmaker Mary Feidt)

The

GREAT
SPRING

Writing, Zen, and This Zigzag Life

Natalie Goldberg

SHAMBHALA
Boulder
2016

Shambhala Publications, Inc.
4720 Walnut Street
Boulder, Colorado 80301
www.shambhala.com

9 8 7 6 5 4 3 2 1

FIRST EDITION
Printed in the United States of America

♾ This edition is printed on acid-free paper that meets the
American National Standards Institute z39.48 Standard.
♻ This book is printed on 30% postconsumer recycled paper.
For more information please visit www.shambhala.com.

Distributed in the United States by Penguin Random House LLC
and in Canada by Random House of Canada Ltd

Designed by Steve Dyer

LIBRARY OF CONGRESS CATALOGING-IN-PUBLICATION DATA
Goldberg, Natalie.
The great spring: writing, zen, and this zigzag life /
Natalie Goldberg.—First edition.
pages   cm
ISBN 978-1-61180-316-7 (hardcover: acid-free paper)
1. Authorship. 2. Zen Buddhism. 3. Creative writing. I. Title.
PN145.G634 2016
808'.02—dc23
2015008186

For Baksim and Pearlie
with Love

CONTENTS

Losing
131

Leaping
167

PREFACE

People come up to me and say, "I love your book."

Mostly I know what they mean, but I become difficult and a bit ornery. "Which one?" I ask. "I've written fourteen."

I ought to feel grateful that I'm still being read, that my work has continued, and simply take in the pleasure that I might have helped someone with the early inspired energy of *Writing Down the Bones,* my first book on practice.

It is auspicious that with *The Great Spring* I have returned to Shambhala, its publisher. Like a big circle closing, the arc is completed. The thirty-year-anniversary special edition of *Writing Down the Bones* and this new book will be released at the same time.

I joke that big brother Bones will introduce the public to little sister Spring. But in actuality *The Great Spring* holds a more mature knowing, saying in an even clearer, more experienced way what is important. I have searched through these stories to find answers—if answers are ever possible—about who I am and who I have become, standing on the ground of being, driven by the practice of Zen and writing.

There are many ways to manifest our true life. In *Bones* I promised to continue. Here are some of the ways I have done so. Please join me in this deep practice of honoring all of our moments. I cannot do it alone. We are here, but not forever.

INTRODUCTION

Fat Robins Arrive

"Listen to the rain," instructs my ninth-grade English teacher, Mr. Clemente, one March afternoon as he flipped off the lights at the beginning of class. There was to be no essay to write or any test on rain. He simply wanted us to listen. We could even put our heads down on our desks if we wanted.

For a few minutes in the regulated school day, we experienced a moment of space, a recognition that something existed outside the classroom. A torrent was hitting pavement and bouncing, sinking into grass, pounding on the window. It was an acknowledgment that an element unknowable and mysterious could be encountered with our senses without referring it to our thinking brains. I felt and smelled rain. It coursed through my blood.

After six minutes Mr. Clemente switched on the light and we abruptly moved into analyzing *Portrait of the Artist as a Young Man,* removing ourselves from the true origin of inspiration: a rootedness in the body and the breath. Though Joyce imbued those pages with essential connections, we dissected his novel rather than staying close to it.

Perhaps the power of those six minutes was intensified because it was so unlikely in our usual scheduled day, like a dangling clause, unrelated to the rest of the sentence. Though I did not pick up a pen and attempt to write a word until I was twenty-four years old, the true heart of a writer was born in me that day. From then on, dreaming became legitimate. Intuiting something beyond the ordinary, yet at the same time smack in the familiar, eventually grew into my life's work. That one afternoon—a Wednesday—liberated me. The downpour was mine.

And isn't that the writer's task? To claim experience, bring it back, express it, not let it pass into oblivion. It's a physical activity, coming from the whole body—lungs, shoulders, hands, kidneys—and from beyond the corporeal. From memory, vision, imagination, the fusing of what is and what isn't, a coalescing of time.

I have dedicated my life to the practice of writing and Zen. The two naturally went together, became inseparable. Through the seen the fine edge of the unseen revealed itself. Writing became religious. The place to encounter oneself, to anchor all the running thoughts and interconnections. Through writing I grew strong-minded, not stubborn. I stood close witness to our aching, inspired living. The act of pen on paper, or two hands on keyboard, rendered a practice of confidence, a training in waking up.

I studied Zen from 1978 to 1990 with a Japanese Zen teacher living in Minneapolis. His name was Katagiri Roshi. From all the early-morning, all-day, weeklong practices—the bowing, chanting, and general fierce regimentation and challenge—and from the years of practice since my time with Katagiri Roshi, I found the heart and dedication that allowed me to give my life to writing.

From my time with Katagiri Roshi, I came away with three clear statements that have created the spine of my long writing life:

1. *Continue under all circumstances.* No excuses.
2. *Don't be tossed away.* If your kid falls and needs stitches, write in the waiting room. If a teacher tears your work apart, learn from it. Be steady. Don't forget your direction and path.
3. *Make positive effort for the good.* Roshi told me this when I was going through a divorce. Positive effort doesn't mean hauling a mountain to Iowa. Sometimes it just means getting out of bed and brushing your teeth. Even if you write about rape, racism, poverty, cancer, it's a positive act. You are speaking out; you are standing up.

Being a writer is not easy. Layers of skin are yanked off. People often don't like what you have to say. Roshi's three dictums gave me a backbone.

Four of Jack Kerouac's *List of Essentials* from his *Belief and Technique for Modern Prose* that provided spirit for this path are:

Accept loss forever.
Be submissive to everything, open, listening.
No fear or shame in the dignity of your experience, language, and knowledge.
Be in love with your life.

The two together—determination and heart, practice and spirit, Katagiri and Kerouac—bestow on us an essential core for a long life of good work and a strong foundation for facing criticism, resistance, boredom, and the transience of mood and desire. We learn to continually show up.

The title *The Great Spring* signifies the great rushing of energy that arrives when you think no life will ever come again. A spray of vitality breaks through: that early yellow-flowering forsythia bush sprouts. Fat robins arrive—you wonder where they've been—and the low moan of the pale-gray mourning dove sitting on the telephone wire fills the air.

I've lived into many beautiful springs, but none ever felt as miraculous as the Minnesota spring. After a northern winter of forty below, you feel certain nature is dead dead—for good. Then the power of life shoots up through elm, birch, and willow, and small crocuses pry open the frozen earth. How can this be?

Spring is a force—impersonal, potent, available to all. Not orderly, not calculable—more like the rain shower I listened to in that English class.

February 2014 in New Mexico was surprisingly mild—in the fifties day after day—while the rest of the country, even Atlanta, was slammed with abnormally cold weather. But my home in Santa Fe might as well have been the Arctic. My hands and feet continually felt like ice, and nothing warmed them. I had received hard news about my health. My heart felt halted by the diagnosis. At night no sleep came. I lay in bed blank minded till dawn. My shoulders were hunched and rounded. I felt the certainty—the inevitability—of death. Yet February turned into March, March into April.

In Zen, the Great Spring is a way of describing enlightenment. Obstructions shatter. Pain cracks open. The previously resisted truth releases. An acceptance of transiency flows through. The Great Spring includes everything; nothing ignored, nothing passed over. No one is so odd that anyone is left out. In this huge terrain, we can find ourselves.

In this book are some of the ways I have found myself—breaking open some of the old strictures of Zen, finding new ways to be alive.

In *The Great Spring* I offer an invitation to enter into a larger, more intimate territory, to commune as fellow reader, writer, explorer, teacher, human being. It is also an invitation to notice, embrace, and record those moments that move us forward—even when the path is not direct. To live a creative life is to search and wander, zigzag and leap, but then to return our pen to the page, again and again, and to reflect.

All of us will die someday. This is not morbid. It is a wedge into fresh life. Finally we look at death—and life—like the old woman at the crossroads in the ancient Zen story. Two lost, wandering monks approach her and ask her the way. She points and answers, "Straight ahead."

Searching

Often I ask:
Was it worth it
to dedicate yourself so completely?
The answer
No

Then I remember:
I saw inside the night sky

I

On the Shores of Lake Biwa

I

I wanted to go to Japan. But Japan was far away. I'm terrible with languages. When I tried to learn short Japanese phrases, it sounded like I was shredding coleslaw with my tongue and not budging one inch from Brooklyn. Plus, all the words of that island country were written in kanji. I wouldn't even be able to decipher signs.

People assured me that everyone in Japan learned English in school. "No problem," they said. I'd studied French for eight years, and all I could do was conjugate the verb *to be*. Better to just spend my days on Coney Island—I knew where the hot dogs were.

But I had a writing student who had lived in Japan for several years. She generously contacted a Japanese couple, and they agreed to take me around Kyoto. They spoke good English, so I could ask questions.

My girlfriend, Michèle, and I had been there a week when Kenji and Tomoko picked us up at the hotel. I'd already felt isolated, walking down crowded streets, peering into unknown

3

temples. I often found myself towering over a young man or woman, asking something and receiving giggles behind polite hands. The Japanese might have learned English in school, but they were too shy to speak it.

"They grind their own beans here," Kenji said as he drove us to a coffee shop.

The smell cleared my sinuses. I rarely drink coffee—I have enough trouble sleeping. But at this moment, I was so elated to speak to a native, not to feel so alone, that I ordered a shot of espresso.

The four of us sat at a small square table, elbow to elbow. "So how do you know English so well?" I asked.

The white cups were placed in front of us. I took a sip. The black blend cut off the top of my head. My eyes darted around the room. No tea, cookies, buns, rolls, rice cakes. Zen purity had been translated into a single-taste caffeine shop.

Kenji explained, "We lived in England for four years. I was getting a PhD in philosophy."

"Really? Who did you study over there?" I'd done my master's in Western philosophy in my early twenties. But soon after I discovered Zen, I never thought of Bergson or Heidegger again.

"Immanuel Kant."

"You're kidding. I did my thesis on him. You went all the way over to Europe for Kant? In America we want to study Dogen."

It was Kenji's turn to be dumbstruck. His nose crunched up. "Ugh, no one understands Dogen. He's much too difficult."

Then I let the bomb drop. "I've been a Zen student for more than two decades."

Now Tomoko grimaced. "That's awful. No one here likes Zen."

I had suddenly become peculiar to this Japanese couple.

Kenji said, "Zen monks all die young."

I already knew but asked anyway: "Why?"

"The training's too hard for a human being," he said.

My teacher had died in his early sixties. I could name several other Zen teachers who had died too early. I had hoped it was the difficult shift they had made to American life, but it was the years of knee-aching, backbreaking sitting on little sleep.

The conversation slid into pleasantries. Yes, I was a writer. Yes, my first book had been translated into Japanese.

My cup was almost empty. If I took one more sip, I'd buzz out the window. I threw care to the neon lights above the entrance and put liquid to mouth. I leaned in close. "Can I ask you a question?" They nodded simultaneously.

Michèle rolled her eyes. She knew where this was going. That morning in bed I had had a realization. Maybe I did know a little Japanese after all. In the *zendo* we chanted from chant cards that translated Japanese sounds into English syllables.

"Does this sound familiar?" I asked, and then belted out the first line of the early-morning chant. At this moment in the zendo, our hands would be clasped in front of us. I saw the whole scene unfold as I chanted *Dai sai ge da pu ku* in the coffee shop.

Kenji and Tomoko shook their heads. "Never heard of it." They must have learned that head shake in England. When I shook my head *no* here, everyone looked at me blankly.

"You're kidding," I said.

"What does it mean?" Tomoko asked.

I was too disappointed to be embarrassed. "Great robe of liberation."

They both stared at me.

"This coffee is delicious," Michèle said and downed her cup.

Tomoko and Kenji explained where they were going to take us. All I caught was "famous temples." But I was templed out. At every temple Michèle and I had visited so far, no one was meditating. Just beautiful buildings; ornate altars; and waxed, fine wood floors. I hadn't realized it, but I'd come for sixteenth-century Japan. I was looking for the descendants of Linji and Hakuin. Where were the kick-ass practitioners, like the wild Americans back in the States who were imitating monks we thought were over here? We woke at 4:00 A.M., meditated all day, sewed robes, ate in formal style with three enamel bowls, and had miso soup for breakfast.

I sat looking out the car window, in the backseat next to Tomoko. Michèle shifted the conversation from the dot-com explosion to a list of Japanese authors we'd been reading since we arrived. I perked up. "Yeah, we're reading these prize-winning novels, and it's a surprise how often the plot is around a homosexual or a lesbian. I thought the Japanese were more uptight than that."

Kenji lifted a hand off the steering wheel. "Oh, no, we're used to it—from the monasteries. The boys go in young."

I gulped. Is that what went on in monasteries?

They drove us from one ancient shrine to another, all with indiscernible names. I was young again, dragged from one art museum to another. The afternoon was a blur. My eyes teared. I wanted to lie down and take a deep nap.

"I'm sorry," Kenji said. "We have only one more, but this one is important. You have to see it. Very famous."

Two young girls in navy-blue school uniforms explained the significance of the temple. All of the other visitors were Japanese. Michèle and I politely stood with our hands shading our eyes. We didn't understand a word.

Then one word registered. Hold everything! Did that ingenue on the left say a familiar name?

"Excuse me, Tomoko," I whispered. "Who lived here in ancient days? What's his name?"

She shrugged. Even though she spoke the language, this world was foreign to her.

"Please, help me." I took her hand. "I have to find out."

The student didn't know what I was talking about, even through translation. She handed me the sheet she read from.

"Is the name 'Ikkyu' here?" I turned the paper over to Tomoko. "What's the name of this temple?"

Tomoko slowly pronounced, "Daitokuji."

"Daitokuji! Did this temple burn down in the fifteenth century? Who rebuilt it? Does it say?"

Tomoko looked back at the paper and translated to the young hosts what I was asking. "Hai, hai," they said in unison, nodding.

"Oh, my God."

The thinner girl pointed to a square white building beyond a high stuccoed wall. This time Kenji translated. "She says Ikkyu is in there."

My eyes widened. Here were the remains of the eccentric Zen monk with a wild spirit whose poetry I loved? I imagined him preserved in *zazen* position in his ragged brown monk's robe, the one he wore when hanging out with drunks under a bridge.

My hands curled into fists. I wanted to leap the wall, burst into the tomb room, bow at his feet, and tell him how I'd spent a cold winter and dark spring reading his poems. Those poems had sustained me.

And not just me. When a friend having a hard time would call, I'd say, "Hold on a minute," and grab *Crow with No Mouth*. "Listen to this," I'd say, and I'd read Ikkyu to my friend.

During his life, people were horrified by Ikkyu's unconventional life—he alternated between practicing hard, then frequenting brothels and bars with prostitutes and hoboes. But when he was eighty-two, he was asked to be head of Daitokuji.

7

It was a great honor. He did not refuse. With his tremendous energy, he rebuilt the temple.

The intensity of having Ikkyu nearby was overwhelming. I was afraid that I'd disappointed this great practitioner. He would have leaped over the barrier. He was waiting for me. I think he is still waiting.

II

I left Michèle in Kyoto to travel north by train to Bukkokuji, one of the few Japanese monasteries that were willing to take Westerners and women. If I was going to be in this country, I had to experience a monastery, even if only for a short time.

Michèle and I went over my route many times in the hotel before I departed. The train moved fast, and I was alert to hear Obama (the town in Japan) announced, even though I knew it wouldn't be for quite a while.

To my right out the window was a great gray lake, reflecting the overcast sky. I heard, "Biwa."

"Biwa?" I poked the man next to me. This was very un-Japanese, but the name sparked something, and the train moved so quickly that I had to act fast.

He nodded briskly, not glancing my way. "Hai."

At the age of twenty-seven, Ikkyu, meditating alone at midnight out in a rowboat on this very lake, heard the *caw caw caw* of a crow overhead and was turned inside out.

He was a poet. It made sense that awakening would enter his body through sound. For a cook the ax might fall while tasting a particularly pungent lemon: she would drop to the ground, savoring bitter lemon in all things.

My stop was finally called. I jumped off, clutching my knapsack.

I followed a path through weeds and empty lots into the

monastery cemetery. Often at night monks sat at the gravestones and meditated. It was midafternoon. I was nervous. I kept repeating, *You'll be okay. You've sat six difficult three-month practice periods, and this time it's just a few days.*

The small complex was a hundred yards away, built right up against a hill. I stepped into the courtyard. No one was there.

Then a beefy monk appeared and spoke to me in Japanese.

I shook my head. I understood not a word.

He continued to talk and motion with his hands. At this point Tangen Roshi—I recognized his face from a photo—glided into the courtyard. He was the Zen master of the monastery. He was in his seventies and had rarely left it in the last thirty-five years. He and the head monk (by now I had figured out who the beefy man was) grunted at each other. The head monk grabbed my pack, and I followed him.

Near twin sinks he stopped and pointed to where I was supposed to go while holding out my sack. I took it, walked alone through a set of doors.

Ten thin mattresses were on the floor. Five Japanese nuns with shaved heads lay on some of them. Near the entrance was a small, spare woman—the only other Western female at the monastery—who introduced herself and pointed to a rolled bed. I nervously set out my few things, unrolled the mattress, and lay down. I didn't know what the routine would be, but I knew it would be in silence.

I tried to rest. How did the saying go? Rest when you rest, sleep when you sleep, cry when you cry. Et cetera, et cetera. I could have made the list go on: be nervous when you're nervous, feel your tight chest when you feel your tight chest, want to go home when you want to go home.

I noticed how hot and humid it was. My straight hair was curling. No one else around me had any hair, including the

Westerner. I remembered what my friend who'd been to Japan had said: *There is nothing like the humidity.* For emphasis he repeated himself: *Trust me, Natalie, in all the world, your clothes will not get wetter than in Japan.* Obama was on the sea. I was in for it.

Bells rang. All seven of us sprang up. They put on their robes; I put on my black long-sleeved T-shirt and black long pants. Together we sat through two periods of zazen in the upstairs zendo across the court. I had no idea how long each sitting was. It could have been twenty-five minutes or forty. I was just happy to know how to do something and proud at the end to recognize the chanting of the *Heart Sutra* as it was shot through at a speed no American could follow.

At dinner we ate cross-legged in the dining room in a ritualized style, with three *oryoki* bowls, chopsticks, napkin, and drying cloth. The actual meal was a mush of colors. What hadn't been eaten from breakfast and lunch was consumed at night. What hadn't been eaten from the meals of the days before was also in there. If mold was forming from a week ago, a high boil took care of it all.

At the end of the meal, we fingered thin slices of pickles to clean our bowls, ate the pickle slices and drank the bowl-washing water. The bowls were then wrapped in the lap cloths with a formal knot. I could do all of this, and the Japanese nuns clucked in surprise.

We sat zazen again and went to bed.

I hadn't spoken a word to anyone. I did not know what time we would wake the next morning, but I could rely on the tight structure. *Don't think,* I told myself. *Take care of your life— connected to all life— moment by moment.*

I did not sleep one moment the entire night. I was drenched in sweat.

I think it was 3:00 A.M. when the bells rang and everyone

popped out of bed. I ran the brush one time over my teeth. We were in the zendo fifteen minutes later.

The zendo was a comfort, but not for long. The bell quickly rang again, and people ran down the stairs. Where were they going? I turned around, and everyone was gone. I bolted after them and saw the monks running out the gate. I put on my shoes and dashed after them.

The streets of Obama were quiet. I heard only the swish of my rubber soles. Thank God I hadn't worn flip-flops. I chugged along, but way behind. They turned a corner and I lost them.

We were the Japanese Marx brothers. I headed east on one block; I saw them passing west on another; I darted north at the lamppost. I caught sight of them sprinting south at the turn. I was panting hard. I hadn't run like this in ten years. The sea was to my right as I galloped up an incline. Just as they neared the gate, I caught up. My lungs were burning. My breath was heaving. I was soaked, hair dripping, pants and shirt stuck to my body.

I followed the monks into an empty room, where less than twenty-four hours ago the head monk had grunted at me. Another monk called out a command, and everyone hit the ground flat-out; another shout and we were on our feet. Then we were slammed on the floor again, doing push-ups. I was already one command behind. They were down; I was up. They were up; I was down.

Finally, the exercise stopped. I was a dishrag.

Sunlight crept across the gravestones. I sidled over to the Western woman and whispered so softly—the sound could have fit under a saltine cracker—"Can we take showers now?"

"There are no showers here."

I nodded. I'd heard a rumor years ago back in the comfort of the Minneapolis zendo that baths in Japanese monasteries were taken once a week at public bathhouses.

I sat on a stone step and waited for the next activity. Exhaustion allowed surrender.

The bell rang. We piled into the zendo and sat for one period. Another bell rang and off everyone dashed down the stairs again. This time I walked. I didn't care if the fires of hell leaped at me.

I found the monks in the Buddha hall in *seiza,* kneeling with their legs tucked under them on the hard wooden floor in a single row. A bell rang in another room, and the first person in line jumped up and disappeared. The row of people on their knees slid up to the next place.

I knelt at the end, the last person, the longest wait. My knees felt as though they were about to snap, but I didn't change positions. I crawled behind everyone else each time the first person left. I knew what was happening.

This was our chance to talk to the roshi face-to-face in his small *dokusan* room. I had heard he was clear, that just to watch him walk across a room was inspiring, that he took joy in the smallest things.

What was I doing here with this resounding pain? No one said I had to stay in this position, but everyone else was doing it, and I was stubborn. Dedication no longer mattered, only animal will. What could I say to this man from another world? I had already had my true teacher. He'd died eight years earlier.

My turn came. I got up, entered the dokusan room, did the three prostrations, and sat in front of Tangen Roshi.

He tilted his head to peer at me. I was hopeless. I knew it. He said three English words: *Not long enough.*

I thought, *Thank God.* I was fifty years old. Too old. Too tired. Too dirty.

The gesture was made for me to leave. The meeting was over.

I had the urge to put my hand on his knee, to assure him I would be okay. After all, here was a man who was dedicated to waking us up. I didn't want to disappoint him, but right then I wanted to go to sleep.

That afternoon, after a work period where we beat mattresses and rolled blankets and towels, we had tea and doughnuts, wrapped in cellophane, bought at a local store. I could tell this was a real treat, and I abstained so the monks could have more.

Each day was long. I had no illusions that something big or deep would happen. I just wanted to make it through each day—running, walking, sitting, eating in that single pair of black pants and shirt.

Young monks ran in the halls and pounded big bells that hung from eaves. Even the army knows to take boys early. Only me, only I don't know I'm not young. That is what these days taught me: I was no longer young. How easy it was for me at twenty-six, at thirty-one—but even then I complained. Now I had only a few days left in a Japanese monastery, and I was thankful I would get to leave.

That day did come and there was no formality. No one said, "Oh, Natalie, we loved having you." I rolled up my mattress, deposited my towel and bedding in the laundry room, and slung my pack on my back.

I was thinking how I couldn't wait to return to Kyoto and take a shower when I passed the altar room. I noticed a big Buddha statue and a small, inconspicuous donation box. Though it wasn't necessary to pay anything for your stay, I thought, *C'mon, Nat, you can give a little something, even though these days were no fun.*

I counted out yen. I was not good at figuring out the equivalent in dollars, a hundred and ten to one, too many zeros. I left what I thought was twenty-five dollars.

I followed the path through weeds back to the railroad station. I was a bit early for the next train. I wandered over to the concession stand and eyed the bags of M&M's. A great compulsion overcame me. I bought two. I ripped one open; they were already melted. I shoved the colored chocolates into my mouth, and they smeared over my right hand and around my lips. I had nothing to wipe them with but my dirty black sleeve.

I looked up: one of the monks from the monastery had just entered the station, recognized me, and was walking over. He was dressed immaculately in formal traveling attire. I tried to hide my chocolate-covered hand. He stood in front of me in his platform sandals. He noticed my hand and flashed a warm smile. I felt the color come to my face. He reached into the front of his robe. He pulled out some kind of bar and held it up. My eyes focused. *Almond Joy.* We both burst out laughing.

My train pulled up. I threw myself into a seat near the window and waved. The scenery zoomed by.

All at once yen popped into my head. I hadn't left 2,750—I'd left 27,500. Two hundred and fifty American dollars. I gasped and my stomach tightened. Then let go. It was fine, just fine. I was glad I'd contributed that much.

III

Michèle was out when I got to the hotel, but she was back within half an hour. "I had a terrible dream last night," was the first thing she said.

"Let's go to a nearby café," I suggested.

We settled into a booth at a small lunch place six blocks from the hotel. I strained to see what was on the display shelves across the counter. "Come on, help me."

Michèle almost whined, tugging at my sleeve. If I didn't know her, I would have thought this bad dream was her way of saying she'd been lonesome and needed attention. But she was not like that. The dream honestly perplexed her. She was one of those lucky ones: basically happy.

It was hard for me to close the distance from the monastery to a human dream. "Tell it to me."

She told me a convoluted tale about her mother working in a self-service laundry.

I listened carefully. The waitress placed tea on the table.

I made a stab at what the laundry might mean. "You're getting washed clean of old habits. Even your mother's willing to help?"

"But then why did she have on her nightgown?"

I tried again. "You always love nightgowns. Isn't your mom you?"

Her eyes focused. A light went on. "Yeah." Something settled in her body. She smiled, took a sip from her cup. "So how was your trip?"

Words ground to a stop in my mouth.

"How was the food?"

"Oh, delicious." We both laughed.

The next morning she showed me an English-language bookstore she'd discovered on a street across from the train station. We had our suitcases with us and were heading out into the country in two hours.

I ran my finger along the book spines, then stopped at a thick yellow one: *Musashi* in bold black letters. He was the great sword fighter of Japan. I yanked the hefty book off the shelf. This was his living story in novel form. Even though it meant lugging the 970 pages along on our travels, I had to read it. I carried it over to the cashier.

Japanese trains are exact. Only one headed toward Kyushu, at 11:21. We hopped on. I looked at the countryside as it breezed by, fingering *Musashi* on my lap. I hesitated and then opened the book.

As the train clicked through stops, I traveled deeper into the book. Musashi studied with Zen teachers rather than sword masters. He walked a hundred miles to find this one particular monk hidden in the mountains.

Michèle nudged my arm. "Wow, look at the rice fields."

I lifted my head through four centuries. My eyes were glazed over. "Yeah," I said.

"Do you want one of the *bento* boxes? Someone's coming through our car." She nudged me. "What kind?"

"What kind of what?" I saw the vendor. "Shrimp."

She put the box on my lap, bent to my ear. "My little samurai, you need nourishment for all of your conquests."

I sighed and closed the book. "This isn't shrimp. What is it?"

"I don't know. Try it." Half the time in Japan we didn't know what we were eating. In the monastery I let go of my picky nature, but back in ordinary life I ate only the recognizable rice and some ginger piled at the side. "You finish it." I handed the rest over and charged back into the book. I'm normally a slow reader, but by the end of the day I was on page 208.

We arrived in Beppu in late evening and dragged our bags to the *ryokan*, a traditional inn, and flopped into bed. I reached my arm out of the covers and along the floorboards to feel for the book. I had a flashlight to read by.

Michèle grabbed my arm.

I hesitated. A moment's battle raged in my head. I let go and turned toward her.

The next day at the medicinal baths, a woman in the pool screamed and hissed at me when I entered. I was *gaijin,* the white person who defeated her country in World War II. I grabbed a cup, scooped up the hot water, and poured it over my head. The angry woman heaved her body out of the shallow pool. The thick water dripped from her old thighs and sagging breasts. She grabbed a towel and slammed a door behind her. I wasn't wanted here.

I dried and hurried back to the ryokan. I was now on page 431. No one could beat Musashi. His rivals were dumbfounded by his two-handed method. It was like meeting a hurricane gale in the void. All of their practiced techniques had no effect.

On Tuesday we went by bus to Mount Aso, the famous active volcano. All over the mountain were signs indicating danger: *Don't go farther. It erupts at any time. No saying when.* We walked around, peering into pools. White cement shelters dotted the lower part of the volcano in case rocks began to fly or lava was spit out of the great mountain. The Japanese stayed far away from us. There were no other Western tourists. One old man pointed at us.

"The last bus is here," called Michèle. "C'mon." She waved her arms. She turned and ran to the line forming for the bus. The temperature was dropping. The last person was boarding. I tore after her.

In the last days of our trip, on a six-hour train haul across Japan, heading to Tokyo through Kyoto, Musashi faced his final challenge. He no longer wanted to fight, but this was destiny. Ganryu, the greatest of all Japanese swordsmen, was waiting for him on a small island. Musashi arrived two hours late, a completely unconventional act. Ganryu's eyes shot fire; Musashi was quiet, but an unearthly fierceness settled in him. Both were free from conscious thought as they faced each other.

We had stopped in Kumamoto City to visit Musashi's memorial place. I prostrated myself nine times before his statue. I read the plaque nearby, which had an English translation. Victory was not what ruled him. The Boundless Way, embracing all things, including the sea and the sands, were what moved him. Even his foes were his teachers.

Miyamoto Musashi's actual burial ground was in close range. According to legend he had been buried in full samurai regalia clutching his faithful sword. The last line of the translation: *He died lonely.*

The Japanese liked loneliness. It had a different quality than our dreaded isolation. More like one with the void, alone with the Alone, no longer separate from anything. It was the final compliment to describe him this way.

Michèle nudged my shoulder. "Our stop's coming up."

I didn't lift my head from the book. She nudged me again. I didn't budge. Muscles, flesh, hair, nails, even eyebrows were united into a single force. An enormous shout shattered the instant, and Ganryu's Drying Pole streaked through the air.

Someone above me reached for her suitcase and walked down the aisle behind the other departing travelers, all collecting near the back of the car.

Musashi does the unexpected. Instead of proceeding slowly, he strides boldly like an animal. This artless approach halts Ganryu. The wooden sword rises straight in the air. One huge kick and Musashi leaps high. Michèle looks over her shoulder as she stands in line. I don't move a muscle.

The hell with Natalie. Michèle has her own destiny. Tokyo, here she comes.

The train slides to a stop. The rush of unloading; new people fumble for seats. The whistle blows. The doors close.

Sealed in the power of speed, barreling through the dark, the tip of the Drying Pole cuts through Musashi's red headband. It flies through the air. A smile flits across Ganryu's face. He mistakes the headband for his opponent's head. The next moment his skull is shattered under the blow of Musashi's sword. The island is silent. Only the sound of a winged bird overhead.

Musashi walks the ten paces over to the prone body and kneels. No sign of anguish or regret on Ganryu's face. Only satisfaction at having fought a good fight. This man is the most valiant of all of Musashi's adversaries. Never in his life would he meet another opponent like this. He bows. The battle is over.

I am crying uncontrollably. Nose running, I grope for a tissue I do not have.

But Musashi's victory proves nothing. More people want to challenge him. His only resolve lies in the depth of his heart. He knows the confused mind is a shadow that people beat their heads against.

My head jerked up. Where was Michèle?

My mind ran the distance back to the vague voice — "It's time to get off." The heavy book fell between my knees and dropped to the floor. I couldn't read or speak in this country.

I didn't dare panic. Next stop I'd get off, cross the platform, and board the next train going in the opposite direction. What if it didn't stop where she exited? I couldn't think of that. What hotel? I had no idea. I had to find her.

Musashi never married his lovely Otsu. He was too busy with the Way. *Be Zen now. Get back to that station. Do what you have to.*

With my right hand, I grabbed my bag from the overhead rack. With my left I clutched the book the way Musashi clutched his sword. I joined the line for the stop.

I stood out on the platform among a thousand strangers. Numbers flashed; Japanese was spoken over speakers. I leaped on the next train going in the opposite direction, sat in a seat near the exit. I gauged that it must have been fifteen minutes ago — maybe twenty — since she got off. I held my breath, hoping I hadn't jumped on an express to the heart of Tokyo.

There was an announcement. The train doors slipped open. I jumped off, frantically looking around. Was this even the right stop? I dashed down the stairs, bumping into people, stretching my neck.

There was someone in a green jacket in a row of seats. I ran over and practically jumped into the person's lap. It wasn't her. I backed away from the astonished man's stare.

I was turning in circles. Someone was standing by the cans of tea. Another green jacket. A red bag at her feet. I screamed, "*Michèle!*"

Her head turned. I flew over and grabbed her.

"I waited. I waited for you," she said against my chest.

"I'm here. I'm here," I cried back.

2

Tennis

(for Katie Arnold)

When I cannot sleep I relate the old story in my head—tennis, my first taste of no mind, living on the edge of instinct. I include Jane Makowski, who did not play tennis but beat me every summer in the freestyle swim. I was repeatedly second. I accepted this and went to the courts.

Jane from Queens—short, dark skinned, white smile, curly brown hair, with a bracelet on your left wrist—where are you now? If you hadn't beat me, I wouldn't remember you. I hope you are well. I hope you never smoked, never got breast cancer, had as many children as you wanted, and married a good person who loved you.

It is 3:00 A.M. in a hotel in the Dordogne Valley, where at 5:00 P.M. the evening before, against all reason and instead of dinner, I had ordered a *glace liégeois avec glace café*. The French, when they make coffee ice cream, are serious. The rich, tawny dessert is full of caffeine. I had cursed myself to another sleepless night. Mostly I can't get over the feel in my hand of the dark tape wound around and the heft of the handle, how the grip went down and rooted to my very feet, through the soles of my sneakers, through the asphalt of the court, down to the earth itself.

At twelve I went to summer camp and walked on a court for the first time. All first times after that didn't matter. I held the racquet at an old-fashioned angle—straight arm, muscle bulge hardening below my unbent elbow, open swing, chest undone. Step into it, step back away, come to me, come away, unfurl the white Spalding ball, thumb and four fingers, steady wrist, my age, a dozen years. Camp Algonquin, the only camp I ever went to. My wood Slazenger, bought for twenty-five dollars at the hardware store on Hempstead Turnpike. So long ago, so young.

I loved tennis with every cell, and the amazing thing was I couldn't do it alone. I had to have a partner. I tried the squash walls: the ball answered wrong, came back too fast, too low, too artificial, too alone. I needed others before I knew or could pronounce *loneliness*.

Alone on the court, I'd play with anyone who arrived—bunk 6, the nine-year-olds; the waiters at sixteen; it didn't matter. Just play with me, hit the ball and I'll hit it back—high fly, low slam, curve, slice, skidding, pop—pouring the life out of me.

Did I play with Melvyn Greenspan or Freddie Kornbluth or Irwin Berger at camp? I don't think so. I kissed them through my thirteenth and fourteenth years. Irwin with the long straight nose and red freckles covering his whole body; Freddie, who is probably in jail now; and Melvyn, probably in the gambling racket. But Irwin I bet is a dentist, like his uncle Ira.

In the middle of the night I remember how I visited my grandmother in Miami Beach in December and walked away from the ocean four blocks to where a tournament was being held at Flamingo Park, sat on a green bench between the high iron fences separating the eight courts. I closed my eyes, feeling the *paaa paaa paaa* around me in all four directions from the felted yellow balls hitting in the magnificent center of the strings. I could tell from the sound who could play and who was faking it, who drank too much, who had wrong sex the night before, and whose wife didn't love him. It was all men playing that afternoon, and soon my grandmother would be looking to serve me her boiled plain chicken. To return to family, I tore myself away from the hum in my body, the central hunger in my breath.

At home I grew wan in front of the television. Too easy to use the word *depression*. I was disappearing. At home I didn't care about winning; I gave that up at birth—out of my mother's belly in 1948. At home I surrendered to sadness: my mother shopping at Loehmann's to ameliorate whispers of Auschwitz, my father split open with rage by the taste and excitement of war, and my grandparents with their immigrant dream of American success. But come each green of July and August at Summit Lake in the Adirondacks, electricity bolted through my right hand, all the way down my legs. Against Camp Ticonderoga, Camp Iroquois—the little white savages from the suburbs—I could beat them all.

Whoever invented tennis, thank you.

Who put this aspirin on my tongue? Uncle Venty, who went into partnership with Bob Shurr and a woman from Canada, who insisted on Shabbat, taught us the McGill marching song that I can still whisper some nights when all else fails. *The G stands for grace and gallantry, sons and daughters of the world to be.* My relative owned Camp Algonquin—the only reason I could go.

I found an opening there, not to fame and fortune but to a clarity outside the weight of history and my mother's aggravation. The only thing playing on the field of thought was the swing, the lob, the eye narrowed on the net, the follow-through, the bounce, the splash on the other side. Far away the other campers were playing volleyball, softball. I wore my navy-blue shorts and white T-shirt.

I did not play at home, ever, until my junior year of high school, when I was dying inside. After dragging myself through the unforgiving halls of ninth and tenth grades and into the spring of my junior year, I finally tried out for third singles. The short gym teacher, Miss . . . Miss . . . Miss . . . ; I thought I'd never forget her name. Late in the season she turned in the green seat of the school bus, headed for another game: "And you, Natalie, have never missed a practice." How could I? I had nothing else to do. I'd never go to the junior prom, never have a boyfriend, only two friends—Phyllis Di Giovanni, whose father was a garbage man, and Denise Hodges, whose mother cracked her gum while frying hamburgers over the stove.

I'd come home from games late, everyone at the table eating. I stood at the entrance of the kitchen, green linoleum spread out like an ocean between us. My father paused for a moment, a pickle in his right hand, noticing for the first time that I wasn't there. "Where were you?"

"Tennis."

Head nod. "Eat."

And I joined the onrush of food.

But when Miss What's-Her-Name had turned in the seat of that bus, even more important than tennis, she recognized me. Someone else considered me. The lost girl had a place. She held her own on the court.

I had played Massapequa that afternoon. I won the first match six-love and the second, six-one.

Going home, flushed with victory in the last seat on the bus, I sat quietly looking out the window, seeing my reflection in glass.

Two days later, Farmingdale High played Bethpage. The girl across the court with two long braided pigtails and a cracked front tooth could not return my serve, which seemed as sharp as a broken mirror. Even I was surprised by its speed. My opponent never had a chance. This time I sat behind the gym teacher in the bus going home and noticed the part in my teacher's black hair and how the strands dangled above her shoulders.

In my freshman year in college in Washington, DC, Mark Plotkin, a future boyfriend, saw me on the courts. It was my smile, he said, when I made a good shot, swung hard, the swirl below the right toe of my rubber sneaker deepening.

How did I dare leave tennis behind, drop that true poetry for the one of words? What other things have I left? Minnesota, Ann Arbor, college, graduate school, two literary agents, a dozen houses and apartments, sex with men (though that too was a fine thing), believing Norfolk, Nebraska, was the center of America.

Not so many years from now I'll leave the body behind. Hover unencumbered the way I did in puberty. Only then I had a fine body to reenter when I put the racquet in its wood frame, twisted the screws tight so it wouldn't warp, tucked the two balls into my back pocket, and walked off the court into the scream of summer.

3

A Long Relationship with Zen

More than four decades is a long time to be engaged in one activity. Have I managed to do meditation every day no matter what? No. Have I often experienced states of bliss that kept me going? No. Did my knees hurt? Yes. Did my shoulders ache? Yes. Was I sometimes filled with anger, aggression, tormented by old ragged memories? Yes. Did I burn with sexual desire, crave a hot fudge sundae so bad my teeth ached? Yes.

Why did I do it? What kept me going? First, I liked that it was so simple, so dumb, so direct, so different from the constant rush of our human life. When I sat I wasn't hurrying toward anything. The whole world, my entire inner life, was coming home to me. I was tasting my own mind; I was beginning a true relationship with myself. This was good—and it was inexpensive. All I needed was my breath, a cushion or chair, a little time.

Over the years I have heard much instruction on how to meditate. Recently I listened to someone tell students that it is better to sit for five minutes every day than for an hour three times a week. I thought, *That's good advice.* Then I smiled to myself. There are no prescriptions for a long relationship. Things change. Five minutes every day might work beautifully for three months. But then what if you miss a day or a week? Have you failed? Do you quit altogether? I hope not. But sometimes our minds set up stiff expectations, and when they're not met, we drop the whole thing. This is just the opposite of softening the mind, which we hope will be the result of meditation.

So maybe the first rule we should begin with, if we want meditation to be in our life for a long time, is: Don't make a rigid structure and then chastise ourselves when we don't live up to it. Better to keep a limber mind and develop a tenderness toward existence. We missed a day? We'll begin again the next day. There's no race. Where are we going anyway but right where we are?

But I also want to encourage having a structure. Perhaps this is the second rule: Structure is a good thing. It's easier to return to something solid than to an amorphous intention. So let's begin with that five minutes—that time structure—and even clarify it more: When will I sit those five minutes? First thing in the morning? Right before I go to sleep? When the clock says noon, no matter where or what I'm doing? If a time is picked, it sturdies the practice.

And if we pick a regular place, it deepens the intention. Where will I do it? At my desk before I begin work? In front of the altar in my bedroom? Under the sycamore in the yard?

Structure allows us to drop in more simply without giving monkey mind a lot of space. What is monkey mind? You know. It's the person in us that wiggles around a lot, that is indecisive, changes its mind, never settles, tries to talk us out of whatever we plan to do. It says: *Not today, I'm tired. I'm hungry. I'm worried about my exam. I can't sit still.*

Look around. Is there anyone sitting still except the floors, the walls, the mountains? Monkey mind will have a hundred reasons not to meditate. Structure helps support our urge to do it anyway. A fluid mind keeps the structure from getting rigid. A structure that worked fairly well for three years may suddenly collapse. We have a new job with different hours; we're traveling for two months; our wife just gave birth to a second child and the house is endless chaos.

Maybe the third rule, which includes the first two, should read: Be creative and flexible at the same time that you continue your meditation relationship. Learn to meditate in a chair while sitting in the waiting room of the dentist's office, or in the car as you wait for your daughter to finish soccer practice.

Meditation is about having our large life smack in the center of our everyday life. How do we stay open and continue?

I was at a retreat at Plum Village in southern France when the person next to me asked Thich Nhat Hanh, a Vietnamese Buddhist monk, who was then in his sixties, how he kept his practice alive.

He smiled a wry, sweet smile. "So you want to know my secret?"

She nodded eagerly.

"I do whatever works and change it when it no longer works."

I thought of the small round labels that were handed out to us at the beginning of the retreat. We were instructed to put them in the inside of our shoes. I still have that note glued on the left insole of my turquoise moccasins. *I walk for you.* Every time I put on those shoes in early summer, a gap opens and I remember: I live connected to everyone.

When *Writing Down the Bones* first came out in 1986, I was invited to teach in Selma, Alabama. I was delighted by the thick air and the abundant trees, so different from my dry New Mexico, and I was curious about an author who lived an hour away in the country. She'd just won the Hemingway Award for a first collection of her short stories. She was in her seventies. Unfortunately, my visit was too short for me to meet her, but I had the privilege of speaking to her on the phone.

"Have you been writing all of your life?" I asked her, elated at the victory a writer could still have at seventy.

"I wrote through my twenties and then got married and had a son. I didn't start up again until my sixties, when my husband died."

I was a gung ho writer then, wouldn't give it up for anything. "Well, was it hard? I mean, giving up writing. Did you resent it?"

"Oh, no, I didn't feel bad. All the years I didn't write I never stopped seeing as a writer." She paused. "Anyway, I could never have created anything as fine as my son, David."

I always remember that conversation. Even if you can't write, you can see the way a writer does, notice, take in, digest the details and stories of what surrounds you.

I think this is also true of a life of meditation. There might be periods—a year or even two—when we can't get to the cushion, but that doesn't mean we have to give up. This might be the fourth rule: We can still carry meditation inside, still see and feel as a meditator, but physically practice differently.

This is when I made walking my meditation. In Santa Fe I lived near the downtown plaza and close to cafés. I'd do mindful walking to the places where I wrote. One foot after the other. I'd feel my toes bend, heel lift, hip shift, the weight of placing one foot down and the rise of the other. I'd notice how my feet carried me. Then when I was done with three or four hours of writing, I'd walk some more. I'd join the tourists strolling up Galisteo, left on San Francisco, cross over to Burro Alley. I'd transfer the power of my writing concentration down into my feet. I'd leave the mind of my imagination and land in the mind of the streets. My feet became my focus under the one sky, near parking meters, amid the rustle of cottonwoods, the smell of roasted chilies. Even though I consider writing an inner physical activity, where my whole body is engaged—my heart, lungs, liver, breath—walking grounded me to the physical world around me.

Even now, ten years later, when I pass through Santa Fe I feel the birth of my walking life and have a gratitude toward that city. If you saw me in those years, you saw a woman knowing the present pleasure of a mind weighted down into the soles of her feet.

4

Blossom

I am at a meditation retreat at Vallecitos Mountain Refuge in northern New Mexico with a Zen teacher from Boston I have been working with. I'm on the board of this remote enclave deep in the national forest. Tired of flying across the country, I've arranged for him to teach here. I've driven him in on the twelve-mile dirt road past aspen groves and an old, abandoned original settler's log cabin, through green meadows, and along sheer cliffs. We're in my sturdy 1978 Land Cruiser, an old hippopotamus of a truck with thick tires, rattling doors, and a fierce engine replete with a choke to get it going on cold mornings.

I want to impress this teacher in the hope he'll want to return. He's smart and astute, and I'm taken with his teachings. I've already studied with a Japanese teacher for twelve years and then a Vietnamese teacher for six. He's American, and we come from the same cultural context—for once, at the very least, I can clearly understand the language.

The first day, he tells a story about seeing the hairs around a horse's mouth when he spent a year in silence in the woods of Maine. I settle into deep, still sitting in this rural Southwest setting that I love so much.

The next day he presents us with a koan, a short teaching story from eighth- or ninth-century China that is designed to cut through conditioned ways of thinking, enabling a person to experience one's true nature. My usual response to hearing a koan is stunned silence. My mind stops dead center, full of hesitation. Some truth is sitting right there, but I can't touch it. Like meeting a whale in a huge fish tank. We don't know each other, but the whale is magnificent and is contained in too small a space—the limits I've put on my mind.

But I am feeling frisky and alive—the morning is crisp—and I'm ready to tackle anything. I'm listening closely, but after the first line of the koan, I am lost—I've been tossed into a swamp and I can't get out. I can't even hear the rest of it. And no matter how many times he repeats it in the lecture, I can't follow it. All I get is "flowers are falling" in the ending.

Suddenly suspicious, I separate myself. *These Zen people are nuts.* My father's voice comes to me: *This is ridiculous.* I've met a chunk of stone from Mars and there's no communication.

The rest of the week we work on this single koan. I count the days, the hours, till I can hop on my faithful hippopotamus and gear through rocky dirt roads out of here.

I can hardly mouth and swallow my oatmeal in the morning.

The teacher tries so hard to make us see. On Wednesday afternoon he has us marching around in circles in the noon sun, imagining we are falling blossoms. It has something to do with becoming the thing, with embodying . . . blooms? Buds? Floral designs? The repetitious bouquet print on my childhood wall-paper? Does it mean spring, youth, vigor, decoration, ornamentation? Should I become an interior decorator? I give up.

In an hour I'm supposed to present the koan, demonstrate my understanding to him in a one-to-one interview.

I am a long-practicing Zen student. Mostly in a nonkoan

tradition, but I have my pride. I want to show something, but I'm dumbfounded—and he's also half a friend. You don't want to appear this stupid in front of a friend. And I'm going to. I don't even have a clue. Maybe if I'm 100 percent stupid, that will do the trick. But I'm not 100 percent anything. I just want to go home.

I remember a story Joseph Goldstein told in this very place at a retreat the year before. In Burma and Thailand he had practiced hard under difficult conditions in small rural huts. In 1972, when he returned, he was about to bring a whole fresh lineage of Buddhism to America.

A year or two later he went to a weeklong *sesshin* with the Zen teacher Sasaki Roshi at Bodhi Mandala in Jemez Springs, in my very own New Mexico. Sasaki knew of Joseph's experience and so gave him an advanced koan. In Sasaki's lineage, each student presents the answer three or four times a day. The practice hall heats up as each practitioner strains to figure out the appropriate answer that Sasaki will give sanction to and then pass him or her on to the next koan.

It is the middle of the week and Joseph has humiliated himself over and over in the small meeting room with Sasaki. He can't answer the koan—not even close—and each time Sasaki quickly cuts him off and rings the bell, signaling Joseph to leave. Finally Sasaki takes pity on Joseph and changes the koan for him to one of the most obvious and elemental: "How do you manifest your true nature when chanting?"

Joseph smiles. This one is easy. He knows the answer even before he leaves the room. You just chant. Nothing else. So in the few hours before he returns to Sasaki, he practices in his head four lines from the *Heart Sutra*.

When it's his time again, he settles himself on the *zafu* opposite this Zen teacher. He is about to chant his heart out when suddenly what flashes before him is his fourth-grade music teacher, Mrs. Snodgrass. "Goldstein, when the class sings, you mouth the words. You're tone deaf." And all at once Joseph's voice cracks and he croaks out half a line of a chant and falls apart, naked, exposed.

He looks up. Sasaki is smiling. "Pretty good. Pretty good," the teacher says.

Now I'm sitting opposite my teacher and I'm a squashed duck in my fourth-grade seat. "I don't get it. I just don't get it."

In a flash he jumps up on top of me and pushes me to the floor. I'm lying on my back and he's staring into my eyes. I shrug like a dead horse and say, "I still don't get it."

"No?"

"No." I shake my head.

He clumsily crawls off.

Finally, the week ends. After many good-byes I'm at the steering wheel. The old car has been sitting idle for seven days. I pull out the choke and the motor *vrooms*. We are on our way. Thank God.

He is next to me. I'm driving him out to Taos. Teacher/student roles have been suspended. We are chugging along when the engine stops dead right in the middle of the dirt road.

I start it up immediately. It chugs along for another ten minutes and then dies. People who will leave later will be coming up behind us if we need a lift, but I want out. Besides, what would I do with the old Land Cruiser if I have to leave it in this remote place? I start it up again and it darts forward for another mile. Then another. Each time I have to start it again.

We decide on a plan. Get it to the main road and bank it. Hitch a ride to Tres Piedras, which consists of a gas station on the corner, a diner next door, and a hot-pink adobe across the highway that always says GALLERY OPEN and never is. The gallery has some mean Dobermans behind a chain-link fence, so no one would think of shopping there anyway. The gas station has mostly empty shelves, but they usually sell Tootsie Pops in a cardboard box. I know because I stock up on cherry ones before I head for retreats at Vallecitos. I'm pretty sure there is a mechanic and a garage too, but it's Sunday. Maybe I can ask them to tow the Land Cruiser on Monday. I have it all thought out.

We finally get to the blacktop. I park the Toyota on the shoulder and we hitch a ride.

The woman behind the counter at the gas station points next door. "They're in there. Working on a car. Go ahead in."

What luck.

I step over the threshold. Two burly men, shirts off, bellies hanging over their pants, grease to their elbows, are under the hood of a Chevy pickup. One skinny man missing three front teeth is to the left, mostly giving them advice and also looking under.

"Excuse me," I say gingerly. "My car died on the road. I'm wondering if you could tow it to Taos."

"Sure," the big man on the right says, but none of them looks up. "Leave the keys over on the table." He juts out his arm in the table's direction but still does not look up.

"But wait," I say. "How will you know where to take it? I want it to go to Doc's on Pueblo Sur. Do you know where that is?"

The same big man slowly stands up and turns his greasy hands in a rag. "You mean, Doc is out of jail?"

"Doc in jail?" I've been bringing my cars to him for twenty years. When I'm stuck he even comes up to the mesa to get me. He was brought up in Taos, married his high school sweetheart at sixteen, lives a few blocks from his shop, and now his son

Wendell works with him. Last time he was sick, I bought him a subscription to an auto mechanics magazine. I consider him, with his gentle steady ways and soft smile, a guru of sorts.

The big man sees the horror on my face. "Nah, I'm only kidding. Sure, we'll bring it in to Doc's in the morning." Then he leans over under the hood again and reaches for some wires.

"But wait, don't you need to know who I am?"

"We know who you are."

He must be kidding. "Who am I?" I ask.

"You're Natalie Goldberg. We've read your books."

"You've—read—my—books?" My mouth hangs open.

"Yeah, whatya think? We were illiterate? New Mexico is one big family."

I place the keys on the table and back up, bumping right into the Zen teacher, who is standing in the doorway. He has seen the whole thing.

"Now I'm impressed." He nods, his forehead creased with two lines, and he laughs.

The next time I see the teacher is two days later. He comes over for chicken soup. A large bottle of sake a friend gave as a gift is on the table. I don't drink, so it is full. He drinks the whole thing. I think, *It must be hard to be a Zen teacher.*

Six months later, I hear that he has slept with several of his female students, and his whole spiritual community has fallen apart. For a moment I flash on our interaction in the meeting room. "Do you get it?" he asked, lying prone on top of me. I wonder if he meant something other than the flower koan? But then I decide no. I'm naive, but I trust myself in this case. Sometimes you have to hedge your bets. I'm a teacher myself, and I know the true effort one can make. We all can fail miserably.

· · ·

Now I'm left suspended between the koan, my broken car, and my cry to the mechanics: "Who am I?"

That small troop of practitioners marching about in the high July sun, trying to imitate blossoms, the light off the ponderosa needles, and the two spring-fed ponds where beavers swim still haunt me. It's a long time later and I still carry the whole situation, with no resolution.

But maybe the tip of the pen on this spiral notebook, midsummer, sitting out on a chipped, red-painted Algonquin chair on this portal in Santa Fe, early Thursday morning, is enough. Maybe the clay birdbath ten feet across the way, where a fat robin bathes every morning, fluttering in the high-desert water like a beached skunk, its feathers drenched and close to its body, is enough. Maybe, just maybe, it's enough to give this story over to you, not to hold on to it any longer. To know that spring is robust and fall is the beginning of the colored descent, and there is nothing you can do about either but receive it all and surrender to no perfect answer and allow no conclusion.

What do you think?

Wandering

Black dog lies across my path

So this is it—
Yellow autumn of my fifty-fourth year
red mailbox at the open gate
and no answer anywhere

5

The Great Spring

Katagiri Roshi had been dead for a long time and still I missed him. And I did not know how to complete the relationship that had begun more than twenty years earlier. I was frozen in the configuration we had when he died—he was always the teacher and I would ever be the student.

More than a decade had passed. I wanted to move on, and in order to do that it seemed I had to move back to that northern state of long winter shadows, a place I left fifteen years earlier to plant my roots in Taos, New Mexico. I had to go back to that cold place in order to unfreeze. So in 2000 I moved back, this time to St. Paul, Minnesota, for a year and a half to practice Zen with one of Katagiri Roshi's dharma heirs.

A few months before the move, a muscle in my groin would not let me cross my legs in the traditional zazen position. I forced it and injured it. This did not please me. I'd been sitting cross-legged for twenty-five years, so that my reflex even at a fancy dinner party was to have my legs intertwined on the oak uphol-stered chair under the pink linen tablecloth.

Structure in the zendo had been everything: straight back,

butt on black round cushion, eyes unfocused, cast down at a forty-degree angle. Bells rung on time. Clip, clip, clip. Everything had order. In a chaotic world, it was comforting. Sitting in a chair in the zendo with feet flat on the floor seemed silly. If I was going to sit in a chair, I might as well have a cup of tea, a croissant—hell, why not be in a café or on a bench under a tree?

But I did go every single day—like a good Zen student—except in the wrong direction, not to the Zen center in downtown St. Paul but to Bread and Chocolate, a café on Grand Avenue. I walked there slowly, mindfully, and it was grand. I didn't bring a notebook. I just brought myself and I had strict regulations: I could buy only one chocolate chip cookie. And I ate that one attentively, respectfully, bite after bite at a table next to big windows. I felt the butter of it on my fingers, the chips still warm and melted. In the past, seven good bites would have finished it off. But eating was practice now, the café a living zendo. Small bites. Several chews. Be honest—was this mindfulness or a lingering? This cookie would not last. Crisp and soft, brown and buttery. How I clung. The nearer it got to disappearing, the more appreciative I was.

"Life is a cookie," Alan Arkin declared in *America's Sweethearts*. I fell over the popcorn in my lap with laughter. One of the deep, wise lines in American movies. No one else in the theater was as elated. No one else had eaten the same cookie for months running. I gleefully quoted Arkin, the guru, for weeks after. I could tell by people's faces: *This is the result of all of her sitting?*

But nothing lasts forever. My tongue finally grew tired of the taste day after day. Was this straw in my mouth, this once-great cookie? In the last weeks I asked only for a large hot water with lemon and wanted to pay the price for tea, but they wouldn't let me. I had become a familiar figure. Instead I left tips in a paper cup—and I sat. Not for a half hour or until the cookie was done. I sat for two, often three hours. Just sat there, nothing fancy, among an occasional man chopping away at a laptop; a mother, her son, and his young friends, heads bent over brownies, eating after-school snacks; an elderly couple breathing long over steaming cups; a tall, retired businessman reading the *Pioneer Press*. I sat through the whole Bush/Gore campaign and then the very long election; through the death of a young boy murdered on his bike by the Mississippi and the eventual capture of the three young men who did it for no reason but to come in from the suburbs for some kicks; through the sad agony of the boy's parents, who owned a pizza parlor nearby.

St. Paul was a small city with a big heart. If I was still enough, I could feel it all—the empty lots, the Mississippi driving itself under bridges, the Schmidt brewery emitting a smell that I thought meant the town was toasting a lot of bread but found out later was the focal point of an irate neighborhood protest.

In early fall when the weather was warm, I sat on the wood and wrought-iron bench in front of the café under a black locust. I even sat out there in slow drizzles and fog, when the streets were slick and deserted. After fifteen years in New Mexico, the gray and mist were a great balm.

Sometimes, if I was across the river in Minneapolis, I sat at Dunn Brothers Coffee on Hennepin or the one in Linden Hills. Hadn't this always been my writing life? To fill spiral notebooks, write whole manuscripts in local luncheonettes and restaurants? But now here was my Zen life too, happening in a café at the same square tables, only without a notebook. Hadn't I already declared that Zen and writing were one? In and out I'd breathe. My belly would fill, my belly would contract. I lifted the hot paper cup to my lips, my eyes unfocused.

My world of meditation was getting large. By leaving the old structure, I was loosening my tight grip on my old Zen teacher. I was bringing my zazen out into the street. But who wants to let go of something they love?

In a city of large oaks, magnificent elms and maples, I managed to return to practice Zen at a zendo surrounded by concrete, where one spindly young line of a tree gallantly fought by a metal gate to survive. I'd renamed the practice center "The Lone Tree Zendo." And, yes, I did actually go there early mornings and Saturdays and Sundays, for weekend and weeklong retreats.

I was working on koans. I had to present my understanding to the residing teacher, and it never came from logic or the thinking brain. I had to step out of my normal existence and come face-to-face with a buffalo passing through a window, a dead snake or an oak tree in the courtyard. The northern cold penetrated me as deeply as these koans. No fly, no bare finger could survive—even sound cracked. I was gouged by impermanence.

By the last days of February, even the most fastidious homeowners—and believe me, St. Paul was full of them—had given up shoveling their walks. In early March I looked out my apartment window to the corner of Dale and Lincoln, near posh Crocus Hill, and watched the man across the street blaze out of his old many-floored, pale-blue clapboard house, jacket flying open and unzipped, with a long ax in his hand. Bellowing, he hacked away at the ice built up by the curb. Behind him stood a massive crabapple, its branches frozen and curled in a death cry.

I doubted that my scheduled mid-April, day-long public walking and writing retreat would take place. Where would we walk? In circles around the hallway? My plan had been to meet at the zendo, write for two rounds, then venture out on a slow stroll, feeling the clear placement of heel, the roll of toes, the lifting of foot, the bend of knee, the lowering of hip. We'd make our way through the dank, dark streets of industrial St. Paul, across railroad tracks and under a bridge, to be surprised by a long spiral stone tunnel opening into Swede Hollow along a winding creek and yellow grass, then climb up to an old-fashioned, pressed-tin, high-ceilinged café with good soup and delicious desserts, where we could write again at small tables. I would not tell the students where we were going. I would just lead them out the zendo door, past the Black Dog Café and the smokers hunched on the outside stoop, near the square for the Lower-town farmers' market.

When the first miserable weekend in April came, I looked at the roster of twenty-four faithful souls who had registered for the writing retreat. Two women from Lincoln, Nebraska, were flying in. A woman from Milwaukee—a six-hour drive away— was leaving at 3:30 A.M. to make the 9:30 beginning. Such determination. *Only in the Midwest,* I thought. I noted with delight that Tall Suzy and her friend from Fargo were coming. She'd studied with me back in New Mexico. Mike, the Vietnam vet from Austin, Minnesota, was driving up too. I nervously fingered the page with the list of names.

The workshop date was the Saturday before Easter. The day came and, miraculously, the temperature was in the low sixties. I hustled over early to Bread and Chocolate to grab a cookie and touch the recent center of my universe. I arrived a few minutes later for class. Everyone was there and silently meditating in a circle. I swirled into my place.

"We are going out for most of the day. You'll have to trust me. Remember: no good or bad. Just one step after another. We'll see different things. This is a walk of faith."

After brief writing sessions we bounded outside, eager to be in the weak yet warming sun. But the deserted weekend desolation

45

of industrial St. Paul sobered us. One step after another. This was a silent walk, so no one could complain—not that a midwesterner would do such a thing. But I, an old New Yorker, had to shut up too. I couldn't encourage, explain, apologize. We just walked bare-faced on this one early-April day, slow enough to feel this life.

Over the still-frozen ground to the tracks, crushing thin pools of ice with our boots. A left foot lifted and placed, then a right. The tunnel was ahead. Through the yellow limestone spiral, built in 1856, a miracle of construction that seemed to turn your mind. Eventually we all made it through to the other side, to sudden country, the hollow, and the sweetness of open land. Long pale grasses, just straightening up after the melting weight of snow, and thin, unleafed trees gathered along the lively winding stream.

We had walked an hour and a half at the pace of a spider. I'd forgotten what this kind of walking does to you. You enter the raw edge of your mind; the naked line between you and your surroundings drops away. Whoever you are or think you are cracks off. We were soul bare together in the hollow, the place poor Swedish immigrants inhabited a hundred years ago in cardboard shacks.

Some people went down to the stream, put their hands in the cold water. I sat on a stone with my face in the sun. Then we continued on.

We didn't get to the café until almost two o'clock. The place was empty. We filled the tables and burst into writing. I remember looking up for a moment into the stunned faces of two people behind the counter. *Where did all of these people suddenly come from? And none of them are talking?*

I'd forgotten how strenuous it was to walk so slow for so long. I was tired.

When it was time to leave, I had planned to follow the same route back. The students shook their heads and took the lead, almost at a trot. A shortcut across a bypass over noisy Interstate 94 to the zendo. We arrived breathless in twenty minutes.

Back in the circle, I inquired, "How was it?"

I looked at them. My face fell. I'd been naive. They had run back here for safety. That walk had rubbed them raw. One woman began: "When we reached the tunnel, I was terrified to go through. It felt like the birth canal."

Another: "I didn't know where it would lead. I looked at all of us walking like zombies and began to cry. I thought of the Jews going to the chambers."

I remembered two kids in the hollow stopping their pedaling and straddling their bikes, mouths agape, staring at us. "What happened to you?" they asked.

I checked in with my own body right then. I felt the way I do after a five- or seven-day retreat, kind of shattered, new, and tremulous. They were feeling the same.

One woman said, "I physically felt spring entering the hollow. It was right there when I slowed up enough to feel it. I opened my hand and spring filled it. I swear I also saw winter leaving. Not a metaphor. The real thing."

They were describing experiences I'd had in the zendo after long hours of sitting. But I'd thought only within the confines of those walls, and with that cross-legged position I loved, could certain kinds of openings occur.

I wanted to cling to the old structure I had learned with my beloved teacher, the timeworn way handed down from temples and monasteries in Japan that he painstakingly brought to us in America. Yes, I loved everything he taught me, but didn't the Buddha walk around a lot?

What I saw now, with these students as witnesses, was that it was I who had confined my mind, grasped a practice I learned in my thirties, feeling that nothing else was authentic.

I told the world that writing was a true way, but even I didn't truly believe it. I only wanted to be with my old teacher again when I came back to Minnesota a year ago. I'd returned to St. Paul, it turns out, not to let go but to find him. Like a child, I never really believed he'd died.

Zen was suddenly everywhere—in the notebook, on the corner, in the moon and lamppost. What was Zen anyway? There was you and me, living and dying, eating cake. There was the sky, there were mountains, rivers, prairies, horses, mosquitoes, justice, injustice, integrity, cucumbers. The structure was bigger than any structure I could conceive. I had fallen off the zafu, that old round cushion, into the vast unknown.

I looked at these students in a circle. This day we were here and we experienced that we were here.

I could feel Roshi's presence. I thought he had died. No one had died. And in a blink of an eye none of us were here. Spring would move to summer, and if we were very lucky, no one would blow up the world. Maybe there were other summers and other winters out there in other universes.

If we can sit in a café breathing, we can breathe through hearing our father's last breath, the slow crack of pain as we realize he's crossing over forever. Good-bye, we say. Good-bye. Good-bye. Toenails and skin. Memory halted in our lungs: his foot, ankle, wrist. When a bomb is dropped, it falls through history. No one act, no single life. No disconnected occurrence. I am sipping a root beer in another café and the world spins and you pick up a pen, speak, and save another life: this time your own.

Early the next morning at 3:00 A.M., one of those mighty midwestern thunderstorms broke the dark early sky into an electric yellow. I gazed out the cold glass pane. Either in my head or outside of it—where do thoughts come from?—three words resounded: *The Great Spring*. The Great Spring. Together my students and I had witnessed the tip of the moment that green longed for itself again.

6

Wrong Way

The Stone Lions are an ancient ruin six miles from the head-quarters of Bandelier National Monument. You go up a cliff to a mesa; you go down and up to another mesa; and again you do this through scrub oak leaves turning in the October light and piñon and juniper that grow slowly and never turn color. Then you repeat the up and down of gaining four hundred feet and dropping down again three times on the way back. It's a twelve-mile hike. You have to leave early to go round-trip before the sun sets at six.

The Stone Lions are rarely talked about. It's a hike you have to build up your resolve—and reserve—to do.

A poet I met in Taos fifteen years ago told me about it. Just the name Stone Lions drew me in. I imagined two actual stone animals standing alone against the empty sky. I knew this was not true, but it fed my imagination and it built my desire to go there.

But it was always summer, too hot, or winter, too cold and not enough daylight, when I thought of it. When you live in a place, you seem to think you have endless time to see the sites—

and you never go. New Yorkers don't go to the Empire State Building, but Kansas tourists can tell you all about it.

I have just returned from three weeks in New York and my head is filled with art exhibits, subway stops, the Frank Gehry building in Chelsea, a Horton Foote play, corned beef sandwiches, sidewalks, the Hudson River. Then Robin Becker, the poet, calls. She is visiting Taos from her small town in Pennsylvania. "Hey, do you want to meet Tuesday and hike to the Stone Lions?" I say yes without considering my weary, out-of-shape body. We will meet at nine, when the park opens. It's a two-hour drive from Taos and fifty minutes from Santa Fe, where I now live.

I pack egg salad and turkey sandwiches, a bag of cashews and raisins, a brownie, dried mango slices, a banana-strawberry smoothie and two quarts of water. I dress in light layers. When we connect in the parking lot, we slather sunscreen on our face and hands. We deposit ten dollars at the visitor center to get a rare map of the area. The ranger cautions us that the trail is not marked well and that we'd better get another quart of water at the food concession to bring along.

I am jazzed. Consequently, I don't pay close attention as we begin to ascend the switchbacks of the first mesa. I'm exhilarated by the land and look at the sky. So big. Home again after being in New York.

We have just passed through the main visiting area of Bandelier, a narrow, long canyon with a stream running darkly through it. The stream is the key. Water in the Southwest is a precious commodity. It's why ancient Anasazi cliff dwellings are found in the canyon walls, and the ruins of a whole pueblo are at the base. At the end of the thirteenth century, the Anasazi abandoned the area, and no one knows why. Speculation is that the stream dried up, but now it's here, feeding the roots of tall ponderosas, which give off a sweet vanilla smell.

I'd gone to New York to reclaim my own homeland. I had fled at eighteen from an unhappy childhood and never returned, except for occasional short trips to visit family—now gone—or to teach a weekend workshop, see an editor, wolf down a pastrami sandwich like a refugee on the run—always antsy to get out of there. This time, at almost sixty, I traveled there to honor the New York in me—and if I was honest, to check out the possibility of moving back. I was lonesome for old roots.

I listened to my Brooklyn friends' accents and asked myself, uncomfortably, *I sound like that?* I'd been gone forty years and still dropped letters on words and added them where they didn't belong. "Bra" seemed ridiculous if not pronounced with an extra *r:* "brar." *We sound retarded,* I thought. And there was this nasal quality, like we always had a cold. And why did we have to talk so loud?

The corker was when I entered a barbecue joint with a friend. We stood in line to order, and someone would come to our table with the food. "Susie, I have to run to the bathroom. Order for me." I tell her what I want.

I am on the toilet seat with my pants around my ankles when there is a loud knock. "Natli, do you want wet or dry brisket?" she screams through the door. I decide to ignore it.

That method does not work. "Which one?" she yells again.

I succumb. "What's the difference?"

"Wet has fat; dry is lean."

"I don't know. Wet." She goes away.

Immediately another hard knocking. "Anyone in here?" a young boy calls.

"Yes," I say.

"Hurry up. I have to go," he calls back. He turns. "Mom, why doesn't she come out? When is she going to be done?" The mother does not hush him. He bangs and calls out till I explode out the door and they scurry in.

This lack of privacy is part of what I ran from. I wanted space. But I have made a vow to claim it all once again.

And the truth is I find a sweetness here under the gruffness. An old man walks me to the subway stop. He's concerned I will not find my way. A middle-aged woman repeats directions to Spring Street slowly. Sweetness may not be the word—a concern, a care. The sweetness is mine. I do not have to fight this place anymore.

We reach the top of the first climb. There are two trails. Without thinking, we take the left one. We are too busy talking. Robin's mother has died recently. "For the last twenty years I spoke to her on the phone every day."

"You're kidding." When my mother was alive, we spoke about four times a year.

"Twenty years ago my sister committed suicide. We became very close after that. They stopped thinking I was mentally ill for being a lesbian. I was all they had left."

"Robin, I think we went the wrong way." We'd been walking parallel to the edge of the mesa. "We need to be walking west—across this."

We turn around. We can't find another trail and begin to bushwhack. "I'm sure we'll find it," Robin says.

"Can you remember? We can't lollygag. We have to get back by sunset."

"I know we have to head for the next canyon."

We weave in and out of endless piñon and juniper, pass big ant mounds of tiny quartz pebbles.

"You head that way." I point. "I'll go this, and for sure, we'll cross the path." I go two hundred yards. "I found it. I found it!"

Robin scurries over. "This must be it." There are no other paths anywhere.

I am relieved. When you have a path, you don't have to think. You're secure in your direction.

After twenty minutes she says, "We should hit the edge soon."

"I don't see any edge." But we keep going.

It is eleven now. The sun is climbing. I take off my wool sweater, wrap it around my waist and glug half a quart of water. We keep walking faster to get to that edge.

"I think we're on the wrong trail," I say after another ten minutes. "Give me the map." It's the first time we've looked at it since we started.

"Do you want to go back and find the right trail?" Robin feels responsible. After all, she has hiked this twice—many years ago.

"It's too late now to make it there and back." I run my finger along a line. "I think we're headed on this one." I try to drain disappointment from my voice. "We can hike here and maybe see the Rio Grande."

Our pace becomes more leisurely. In mileage it's as long, but the ground is all level and we stay atop one mesa. *What a hokey hike,* I think, but don't say anything.

Robin first came to New Mexico on a Wurlitzer Foundation Fellowship in 1978, when she was twenty-eight, and fell in love with Taos. After that she came almost every summer through the eighties. She'd finish her teaching job and hold her breath till she was on the plane to return to New Mexico. She'd always come back alone, jeopardizing relationships. Who was this third character—this land? Many of her lovers from Cambridge had no interest in the dry dirt. *Where was the ocean?* they wondered. She was an instructor in writing at MIT. Then she moved on to Penn State, eventually landing a full professorship, and came west less frequently.

She stayed at my solar beer-can and tire house on the Taos mesa in the early nineties for two summers when I was on retreat. We used to have discussions about her giving it all up and moving out.

"How will I make a living?" she asked. "I'm a poet."

I entreated her to take a chance. She could become a short-order cook, a landscaper, a house painter. See what evolved. "Everyone in Taos makes up their life."

She always said she couldn't.

We reach the spot where we can see the Rio Grande winding green and slow four hundred feet below. Shallow in this part, sandbars appear in the middle.

I'm a bit cheered. We perch on rocks and gaze down. "Let me see the map again."

I look closely. "Hey, look, we can hike down and walk along the river." Halfway down the descent the black map line turns to brown. I look it up on the symbol chart.

"Unmaintained." I follow the brown line. "We can end at Frijoles Canyon and hike up through Big Falls. It's gorgeous. I've done it tons of times."

"I don't know. We could get lost. What if the trail gives out?"

"No worry. We can follow the river. We can even walk in it if we need to. It's not deep." This was the wrong thing to say. I glance over at her and she's aghast.

Suddenly my aching feet and the small of my back where the weight of the backpack shifts don't bother me. I'm hungry to get down there, excited. "C'mon let's check it out."

The path gets rockier and is descending not the way the map says. But who cares?

"Hey, Robin, have you ever read Stegner? He's a Western writer, really good."

"I've heard of him," she says.

"He wrote this book *Angle of Repose*—it won the Pulitzer. It's a thick book and halfway through you want to quit, but you keep going. It's about easterners who move west—Idaho, I think—but they are always writing to friends and relatives back home, thinking they'll return. And every time they go back, they feel uncomfortable. It doesn't work. They don't realize how they've changed—"

"Nat, I want to go back. I don't think this is right."

"C'mon, just to that curve. I know where we're going. We can't get lost." I continue about Stegner: "They've become western without knowing it. They never go back, but they keep looking back." I'm sailing along, high on adrenaline.

"Nat, I want to go back. I don't see a trail down there."

The ground has turned white and steep with loose shale, but it's definitely negotiable. We can bushwhack down this arroyo.

"I'm afraid I'll twist my ankle. I don't see the river. We're in the wrong canyon."

"See that line of color? That's salt cedar. It only grows along a river. The river's down there. C'mon." I can see rows of new green and pink. Now I'm like a horse sensing the water. My nostrils are flared, flanks ready to charge ahead.

Robin digs in her heels way above me. I have never been hiking with anyone who doesn't like an edge of the unknown, a little danger.

"We won't get back before dark."

Who cares? I think. I've never huddled in these canyons through the night, but it probably won't drop below thirty-two degrees. I'm in my T-shirt now; I've shed my long-sleeve shirt, as well as my sweater. I can't imagine being cold.

She calls out again, "I can't do it."

I close my eyes and gulp in a long breath. We could go our separate ways.

I breathe out. I can't leave her. I heave my pounding heart around and climb toward her.

"You'll never want to hike with me again," she says.

"Yes, I will. Nice safe hikes. Ones I've been on before." I reach her.

"You go first," she says.

"Afraid I'll bolt?" All the wind is out of me. The climb is steep. My calves burn. We don't speak.

"You're braver," she says after a while. "I need more security."

"It hasn't been easy," I say. "I had to make my own way. I had no family, no support behind me."

"But when it was tough, you had grit."

"There's a plucked chicken deep in me. The powerful one writes a book, and when it gets published, she's on to something else. The plucked chicken is left to face the crowd."

The way back is longer than I thought. We get lost again and end up coming down a different switchback, with the sun resting on the rim. Eventually we reach the visitors' center.

"I'm low on gas," I tell Robin. "Can you follow me out? There's a station in White Rock." But first I want to linger among the trees in this deep old canyon. Robin wants to hurry along before there's no light.

We drive up the long two-lane highway, away from the secret curve of ancient habitation, into familiar lights, toward a broken pizza sign up ahead.

I pull into the corner station. "Wait one moment while I run to pee."

When I approach her car, she is listening to a CD course on classical music. It's playing Brahms.

"Listen to how beautiful this is." She gets out of the car and we hug. "Let's keep in touch," she says, "and don't forget to fill up."

After she pulls away, I feel a great longing to be in Taos again but turn my car toward the thousand lights of Santa Fe.

On the radio, *All Things Considered* is interviewing a colonel in the army who gives legal counsel and defends military privates. Several people vouch for his supreme integrity. Then he speaks. He's quitting after twenty years of service. "The legal system is a sham now," he says, "especially Guantanamo." He defended a fifteen-year-old who confessed to killing an American soldier only after they chained him into bent-over positions. Every time he fell over they lifted him up. After five or six hours he urinated on himself. They threw Lysol on the floor and used his body for a mop. Then they stood him up again and left him.

I can't believe what I'm hearing. I knew this stuff was possible. I'd just read *Imperial Reckoning,* about what the British did to the Mau Mau in Kenya, but this was my country. The announcer says he couldn't find anyone who would confirm the torture.

The colonel says that boys are returning from Iraq with PTSD and are discharged from the army as crazy. He says, "We did this to them. We need to help them, not reject them."

My beloved grandfather often repeated to me, "You don't know how good it is here. There is nothing like America." He was a Jew who ran from the Cossacks. I inherited his love of this land and was even learning to embrace all of it—the East and the West, which he did not know.

I slid into town, making a left onto the night street, knowing that all of us are at a cliff edge and the trail is no longer in sight.

7

Archer City

I

On the two-and-a-half-hour drive north from Dallas, the ride gets continually more rural until you think you are lost, or certainly nuts to imagine finding something. Even the few cows are bored out of their minds. And the road narrows even more. My friend next to me wants to turn around—"There's nothing here."

But I know there is. Archer City is where Larry McMurtry was brought up. The writer I admired most in my beginning years of putting pen to paper. And that admiration stayed with me, held steady.

I read *Leaving Cheyenne* for the first time in the early seventies, when I was living in a small adobe with an outhouse and no running water in Talpa, New Mexico; I gave it a second read four years later in the Bahamas, lying in bed with a terrible flu, while my new husband stalked the bare back of the beaches alone. My husband's father and mother had both just died, within six months of each other, in their mid-fifties—one of a heart attack, one of cancer. While he was going mad with grief, I was transported through the book to the range, to a woman named

Molly and the two men who loved her, Gil and Johnny—I still remember their names.

McMurtry wrote this second book at twenty-one.

My good friend Eddie Lewis got me to read *All My Friends Are Going to Be Strangers,* another early novel of McMurtry's. At the time this one had a university-press publisher and was autobiographical—in feeling, anyway. The main character was in his early twenties and his first book made it big (which also happened to McMurtry), and the book showed the ensuing pain of success, the pressure, the alienation. In the end the young writer is in the river—the Rio Grande—trying to sink his next manuscript, and the pages keep rising to the surface all around him—hundreds of pages. He pounces on them, pushing them down, trying to drown them.

Of his other books I read— *The Desert Rose, Terms of Endearment, Cadillac Jack, Moving On, Buffalo Girls*—some took place in Texas. Some were located in other places.

Eddie's mother, Alberta, had once met McMurtry at a rummage sale in Washington, DC, where she lived. McMurtry owned a rare books store in Georgetown and was always on the lookout for antique books.

In the mideighties, as his hometown of Archer City, the setting for some of his novels, was slowly becoming a ghost town, McMurtry bought up the buildings and made each one a bookstore. One building held books of poetry, another history. He said that whenever an independent bookstore any place in the country went out of business, he bought up the stock and brought the books home. His family herded cattle; he was going to herd books.

I don't remember when I read *The Last Picture Show,* but it was soon after reading *Leaving Cheyenne.* I'd already seen the movie, and this time the film was damn near as good as the book.

Empty time, an almost empty town, a football player, a coach, his wife, a billiard parlor, wind—and a terrible loneliness. Though McMurtry had Archer City in mind when he wrote, I had forgotten that it was also the actual stage set for the movie.

By the time I drove to Archer City, I had been a successful writer for more than twenty years, but sitting there I still had stirrings of longing, gratitude, and homage.

I barely close the car door, heading for some wooden steps on a raised platform in the center plaza. No traffic. No people passing on the sidewalks. Midday sun. Silent enough to hear the flap of a crow's wing overhead. I am physically in the center of a novel I have loved.

At the main office, a young woman, fresh out of majoring in English Lit, attends the desk. "You pick out your books, come back here and pay." She hands us a map.

"Does Larry McMurtry ever show up?" I ask.

"You just missed him. He went home for lunch. He lives down the road." She pointed to the left. "He'll be back in an hour. You'll see his white Cadillac pull up."

I am going to meet Larry McMurtry in the flesh?

I try to act nonchalant. "Maybe I'll pick up one of his books and have him sign it."

"His books are probably the only ones we don't stock. We do that on purpose. He doesn't want to sign."

The only other people browsing through the stores are a single book dealer from Oklahoma and a man, driving through, headed for Louisiana.

I plant myself directly across the street from the office in the floor-to-ceiling poetry building. I run my finger along the book spines, too jumpy to settle into any one poem or poet. I glance frequently out the window across the broad street. No white Cadillac yet. Robert Creeley, LeRoi Jones before he was Amiri Baraka, Audre Lorde, Mark Strand, Anne Sexton. I don't even know what McMurtry looks like. I'd never seen a photo of him—and he never showed up at writing conferences.

A white Cadillac slips across the front door of the office and parks. I grab a book—I can't walk into the office empty-handed.

I cross the street.

The doorknob turns easily. I feel its imprint on my hand. The office is empty but for books along the walls and a man in his sixties, maybe five feet eight inches, nondescript, wearing a white shirt.

"Larry McMurtry?"

He nods, indicating we could sit at the round table right there. The intern had called ahead. He knew there was a visitor who wanted to meet him. He had all afternoon. We are not in New York, not in LA.

He gestures with his hand. What would I like to talk about?

"I read your books," I say.

He waits.

"I love them. They mean a lot to me."

His face is open, listening.

I look down. I look up. "I live in New Mexico. I came here to see Archer City." I can't think. The old litany from childhood rises up in me: *You are nobody, nothing.*

He bends his head to the left.

"Well, I have to pay for this book." I jump up abruptly and open the cover. Seven dollars, penciled on the used flap. I take out my wallet and lay down a five and two singles.

"Thank you." I glance at him across the table. My eyes dart to the chair next to him, the photo behind. "I have to go."

Clutching the book, I run out, find my friend. She has been ready for a while.

"Could you drive?" I ask, and as the car speeds south I whip out my spiral notebook and pen Larry McMurtry a six-page letter—both sides—telling him how I feel about his work, the town, the sky, the trees by the road. I apologize for being unable to speak. My heart was in my throat, I tell him. I pour out everything I can think of, and I can't wait to mail it, to get it out of my hands.

"Why didn't you just tell him you wrote books?" my friend asks.

Maybe I should have, maybe I even did—I don't know.

I never received an answer to the letter. I didn't expect one.

So many years later, I still go over it in my head: I should have invited him to dinner. I should have told him all about my upbringing in Brooklyn—no books on our shelves either. Told him I once rode a horse named Thunder. I should have tried something subtle—handed him a tangerine.

II

Six years later, I return with a different friend, Bill, to Archer City. This time I notice more as we drive north. Through Denton—I love that name—along a long, flat stretch on Highway 380W; past Mr. Porky's, a barbecue joint; past rows of rolled hay in brown winter fields—it is November—with low-hanging clouds. Past three horses, one lying down in the middle of the day, past Jehovah's Witnesses and the Assembly of God, then an unlikely sign for a Muslim cemetery, then a line of quick signs, one after the other, for electronics, tires, pigs for sale, Prairie Estates, ending with a Phillips 66. A patch of suburban brick houses called Highland Hills, oddly displaced, nothing around them. A burned-out double wide, patches of low-growing cacti. Past Bridgeport, population 1,114.

I'm alert, anticipating this visit.

In Jacksboro, about forty miles before Archer City, we stop for lunch at Nana Lou's Kitchen. My friend found this place in an issue of *Texas Monthly*, featuring an article about the state's best small-town cafés.

The waitress—with a thick Texas twang, wearing a pink Longhorns shirt—seats us near a window. Across the patterned curtains, cowboys lasso steers.

I ask her, "Did you know the person from the magazine who did the review?"

"No, only after he called to confirm that we had eight tables." She holds a pad and pen in hand, ready to take an order.

"Have you ever been to Archer City?" I ask her.

"No." She shakes her head.

"Do you know Larry McMurtry?"

She shakes her head again.

"He wrote *Lonesome Dove*."

"Oh, yeah. I just had no idea who came in here."

I glance over at my friend across the table and we both take the exquisite leap—she thinks McMurtry wrote the restaurant review.

Bill orders the chicken-fried steak and biscuits with gravy.

"Oh, so that's what it is," I say when it's placed in front of him. Often when I've seen it on a menu, I've played in my head: Is it chicken? Is it steak? The steak of a chicken? I never thought to ask anyone. Now I know: a steak deep-fried in batter like they fry chicken.

And the gravy is *white*.

I have a patty melt and it is good.

We pass the sign for Archer City: population 1,848.

The first thing we see is the Royal Theater, this time with fresh, sky-blue paint on the marquee. A box of pansies on the sidewalk with the Texas Star emblem on the outside of the box.

We go into the first bookstore building nearest the movie theater. A huge warehouse of ARCHITECTURE, ART, CRITICISM.

Bill finds an out-of-print southern cookbook he's interested in, but it's $120.

I hadn't quite noticed before how carefully categorized under subject every single book is, clearly lined up, shelved in order, but with no file catalog.

We browse for a while and then walk down the block to an antique store, not part of the book complex.

As soon as we walk in, the saleswoman, without our asking, says the McMurtry books are in the back. Obviously, she knows we are from out of town.

We walk straight back and thumb through them. I select a copy of *All My Friends*.

At the register I ask, "Does he mind that you sell his books?"

"I don't think so."

"Do you know him?"

"Oh, sure. We went to school together."

"What was he like?"

"Real smart."

"What's he like now?"

"Strange."

"How?" I'm not going to let her comment pass.

"In the way all writers are strange. I hope y'all aren't writers."

We laugh.

I persist. "How do you mean, 'strange'?"

"You know, standoffish. Keeps to himself."

"Is the town proud of him?"

She hesitates. "No. Well, I guess, he's done a lot for the town."

She tells us his siblings live nearby.

"Is his family proud? What about his father?"

"No, probably not," she snaps out. Then, "I shouldn't say that. His father was an old cowboy. He was really nice."

"Have you read any of his books?"

"No, I'm not a reader."

"Did you like *Last Picture Show* when it came out?"

"I didn't much care for it. I waited to see the TV version, but *Hud* is my favorite." She giggles. "That's because of Paul Newman."

We walk to the main office of the bookstores, where a different young woman shows us a map of the buildings.

I ask her if McMurtry is in town and she says no, he only comes around about once a month.

Bill asks me, "Are you relieved?"

I shrug. I seem to feel nervous even if he isn't here. I bet I wouldn't have been any better the second time.

The young woman tells us the place almost closed a while ago, but Larry decided to keep it open and he's still buying books.

I tell her if she can find my books, I'll sign them, and I give her some categories. Nothing is computerized. She goes off to search on the shelves.

We cross the street again to the poetry and literature building. The books now are almost all rare or out of print. I hadn't been aware of this the first time I visited. Hardcover of *Lucky Life* by Gerald Stern: $70.

Bill and I are both writers—we automatically want to support a bookstore, but we like to handle books, mark them up. Rare books are a different category. We can't find a book we want to spend so much for. I feel odd—and empty. Thousands and thousands of rare books in a vacant town.

We go back across and the young woman says she can't find any of my books.

III

We walk to the Dairy Queen, a half mile down, where McMurtry wrote *Walter Benjamin at the Dairy Queen*.

Bill rolls his eyes.

"We don't have to eat there," I say.

We pass a big brick house that's much bigger and more formidable than anything else around. The house is dark, and clearly no one's there. Some workers are putting up low sections of garden fence.

I point. "This is McMurtry's." I know it from last time.

The DQ is cheery and spacious, with booths lined against two walls.

I tell Bill, "Choose your booth."

He picks the one in the corner. I tell him, "I bet this is where McMurtry sat."

I order a chocolate milkshake. "I never had one here before." I smile at Bill, who scowls and tells me it will be terrible. He orders an Aquafina. I walk around and read plaques on the wall with framed covers of McMurtry's books.

"Well, someone at least recognizes him," I say, approaching our booth.

"Okay," I say, opening my notebook. "One full hour. Tell your story of love. Go."

His head jerks up. "What?" And then he dives in and we both write like mad.

But in the middle I want to stop. I'd written this all before. My story of love always leads to that one omnipresent woman.

". . . the kind of day winter is famous for—half-light and brown fields, but still almost warm-sweater weather, sun setting low to the horizon. My mother died two months ago. I refused to visit her in Florida last Thanksgiving, and I never saw her again but wheezing on her deathbed. I don't have remorse. I tried so hard with her that my gums bled. I couldn't get her to love me, but I didn't give up. I wish I had. I was always trying a new angle, hoping to be free, to be able to say, *Yes, dear mother,* when she snapped at me. I thought I'd figure it out. . . ."

An hour is a long time to write continuously. I watch the clock and veer off in my writing to name boyfriends and girl-friends and stay away from my maternal lineage.

I didn't have the opportunity to meet Larry McMurtry this time, but I was reminded how often writing brings down the disdain of your hometown. Hibbing, Minnesota, Bob Dylan's hometown, didn't understand why he had to move away, why he didn't visit, and but for a few folks—his English teacher included—the people on the Iron Range hated his lyrics as well as his voice. Sauk Centre, Minnesota, disliked Sinclair Lewis after he wrote his first book, *Main Street,* which told the truth about small towns. After winning the Nobel Prize in 1930, Lewis died alone in Italy, some twenty years later, but he asked that his ashes be buried in Sauk Centre, where they disdained him. And I re-membered how his beloved Oxford, Mississippi, called William Faulkner "Count No 'Count."

And here was McMurtry, planting books—rare books, no less—in a town that didn't seem to care.

I was driven to write books in order to find my lost voice, to be seen by people who could not see me. Why did I think books—something I cared for but they didn't—would wake up my parents? They would read my books and we would have the connection I longed for. I thought they would see into my true heart. Here in Archer City, the scenario felt painfully graphic— the chasm of disconnection.

It's what I've come to understand: writing does not bring love—not the original love you want, at least. So many dreams we start out with as young writers. I thought I'd be invited to grand parties where pigs in blankets—something I saw in the fifties—would be served with doilies on silver trays. After all of these years I have seen ne'er a one of those miniature frankfurters.

At this point, I'm sure McMurtry gathers books in his home-town because it gives him pleasure. Finally, there can be no other reason.

I had come back to Archer City a second time so the young Natalie could catch up with the older Natalie. I didn't come to Archer City to meet Larry McMurtry, like I thought. I came here to meet myself, to close the yawning gap, the chasm of hope and reality.

"Wind down," I tell Bill. The hour is up. I'm glad to put down my pen.

Bill reads me aloud his brash, sad, sexy story of love. I tell him I'll read mine on the long drive back.

We pick our way to the car in the unlit dark, walking on the broken cracks and scattered grass along the road.

8

A Student Again

I was on a yearlong sabbatical. My most recent—and, I thought, my best—book had almost broken me.

Longing for that old feeling of lazy pleasure in the hand moving across the page, not sure what would come up, that old sweet experience of discovery, I talked two of my best writing friends into coming along to a writing workshop on the Oregon coast for six days. I wanted to be a young student again and set aside being the one in charge.

On the first evening we were told to go back to where we were staying and produce two typed pages of risky, naked writing, with seventeen copies to pass around. The next day we held our breath as the work of half the class was analyzed, one by one, by two teachers. On Tuesday the other half would go under the microscope. The teachers had been students of Tom Spanbauer. Spanbauer, the author I actually came to study with, wasn't in sight after our initial meeting the first night.

It is widely acknowledged that writing cannot be taught as a chronological step-by-step method and that this workshopping process, which we were doing in class, is the way writing is transmitted in America. Many great writers have been initiated this way. But I grew impatient. I have assiduously avoided work-shopping for the whole of my writing career.

I repeatedly wriggled in my seat like a kindergartener. Where was Spanbauer? How did I get into this, anyway?

But I knew the truth—I was seduced by attention. Tom Spanbauer, whom I admired, had written me a long letter, telling me how he loved my books. It was a lovely letter. Why didn't I leave it at that? Instead of simply writing back, "Thank you; I like your work too," I had to study with him.

But in all honesty I did need help. I was tired of my writing subjects: my mother, my father, a sprinkle of my grandparents; my childhood in Farmingdale, New York; my old Zen teacher; Taos, New Mexico; Minnesota. A nice list, but thirty years of scraping around in it was enough. Of course, you should be able to write endlessly about a single topic, but I was sick of the particulars of my life.

This writer in Oregon had heart and a wild sexual narrative. Originally from Idaho, Spanbauer had lived in a tent at the foot of Kilimanjaro in his twenties. His first question to me on the phone: *Do you speak Swahili?*

This author's second question—when our class met that first evening in the small elementary school used for summer adult art programs—was *Has Zen taught you anything about dying?*

He'd gone around the room in a wool jacket with a white T-shirt underneath, shaking hands, greeting us. Here he was. I had traveled a long way. Maybe it was his nervousness in finally meeting—there'd been calls and e-mails for almost nine months—that produced the raw question blurted out so quickly, which resounded as the true inquiry, the real introduction.

Squished into a third grader's wooden desk, I stammered. Thirty years of ass-breaking meditation practice, and all I could say was, "I've seen some things." Mysterious, very Zen-like, but what the hell did it mean? The author, who had AIDS, nodded.

Exactly what things have you seen? I asked myself, walking back to my hotel that night, feeling outrageously foolish. What did I know about death? Often I walked a tightrope between the void and a desire for a good hamburger.

No, Tom, I don't know shit about dying. Can I get you a glass of water? Sit by your bed when you're sick and keep you company? Give me your hand. Shall I tell you how your work moved me?

At first I thought Tom's novel *The Man Who Fell in Love with the Moon* was pure porn. I put it down. But men and women in the dot-com world in Palo Alto, where I was living for six months, talked about it constantly. I picked it up again months later while visiting my ninety-one-year-old mother in Florida. At midnight I climbed over the railing to the outdoor whirlpool of the senior center and took off my clothes. Normal hours were from eight in the morning till ten at night. My mother paid the fees all year-round and never went. I thought I'd use up a little of her time. I read Tom's book by moonlight. On page 128 I looked up at the still palms standing tall around me, the milky black sky, and exclaimed aloud to the fat frogs, the square lit swimming pool and its ripply little waves, "I have never read anything like this." On that night I swore I'd meet the man who wrote it.

That was spring. Tom's phone was unlisted. I could not reach him.

The following fall I was on a book tour and read in Portland at one of the bastions of the word: Powell's. It was a good audience. In the back stood an old student of mine, whom I was happy to see. When his turn came for me to sign his book and we'd caught up on a few life details, I leaned close and asked, "Do you know Tom Spanbauer? He lives around here."

I still remember the look of surprise on Steve's face. His glasses fell lower on his nose.

"I teach with him," he said.

When I arrived home, I shuffled through a pile of bills and advertisements. I'd been on the road for a month and I was tired. A blue-inked envelope caught my attention. Above the return address: Tom Spanbauer.

I sat down in my living room and ripped it open. Seven pages, handwritten, torn from a spiral notebook. I didn't trust anyone after this tour. My fans didn't want to go where I was going with this new book. I read Tom's words quickly, nervously.

I glanced through my living room's back window. The Russian olives had dropped all of their leaves. Here was an author I admired who admired me. Believing in ourselves is such a fragile thing. I started his letter again:

> Dainin Katagiri Roshi.
> You are so blessed to have loved so well.
> He was a beautiful man.
> Even more beautiful now that I have finished *The Great Failure*. In fact, I probably would not have loved your teacher at all had he not failed so predictably.

Why hadn't I just visited him in Portland, gone to a café and hung out? What was I looking for? I had to go to Cannon Beach and drag my friends Rob and Eddie along?

Rob called me in Santa Fe before we went to Oregon. "Let's stay a week extra and do our own writing retreat, hammer out eight or nine hours a day." Eddie wasn't enthusiastic about the second week. Too much work. He likes good times, and I assured him we'd have tons of fun. Rob found the hotel and registered us in the class.

The ocean in Oregon was freezing. Rob vowed to dive into it at 5:00 P.M. every day.

On the first day of the class, Eddie and I trailed after, wearing our suits, slinging our towels around our necks, but only going up to our ankles. We decided we'd come as lifeguards.

Eddie turned to me. "Listen. If Rob is drowning, we'll do rock, paper, scissors to see who goes in to save him. If we don't like the results, we can do best out of five."

That sent me over the edge. We couldn't stop laughing, our bodies heaving up and down.

Rob appeared, sopping wet and shivering. "It was even colder than I thought."

"Don't worry. If anything had happened, we were right here," Eddie said, and we started that insane laughter again.

My problem in the class was that they didn't say, "This is good"; "This is bad." Each piece had to have a diagnosis. Sometimes it took more than three-quarters of an hour for us to go over two pages of writing.

I glanced up at the alphabet lining the top of the blackboard. Small *s;* capital *S.* Small *h;* capital *H.* I found the *i* and the *t. Shit.* I was hoping to come to Oregon to become a race car driver, a fisherwoman out to sea, to catch a big one, to find a whole new perspective. Not diddle around with everyone's writing.

The teachers did say something terrific that initial morning: "Don't write about what you know, write about what you don't know."

By the end of the first day, Eddie hadn't said one word or offered one thought in class. If someone didn't know him, he would look like he had zoned out. But that's his cover. He watches closely. I challenged him Monday night. "From now on, you have to offer no fewer than five insights in every class."

"No more than five, either," he said, smiling.

On the second day, Eddie said to the writer of a piece we were looking at, "While you know what the story is about, at the same time you may not know everything. Some parts may be in you but not in your consciousness. So your grip on the story has to be loose. Sure, but loose." I flashed him one finger.

He flashed back four—how many more he had to go.

During the break, the writer came up to him. "Did your hand signals with Natalie mean anything about my story?"

More than our writing was laid out on the elementary school desks. Our whole self-worth was being examined. Writers were an earnest lot. It was painful to watch, painful to experience.

That afternoon, Rob madly wrote notes to himself, then to me, shoving the pages across the desktop. "I didn't sleep well last night until about four. Weird dream about school and me teaching the kids who were out of control. I hardly ever have those dreams anymore. Must be these desks we're in and having to pee in the kids' bathroom."

"Let's have Cheerios tomorrow for breakfast," I wrote back.

By the end of the second long, eight-hour day, a creeping loneliness enveloped me as I tried to listen to the endless discussions of each person's work. Restlessness, the struggle against what hurts, raged inside as I sat squished in that small chair attached to my desk. I didn't belong in this class. A thought was slowly dawning on me: I wasn't going to make it through the week.

One student, sitting in the rear of the room, wore a black T-shirt, had dyed black hair, a lip ring, a nose ring, and a pale flat face. He was twenty-three. He never spoke except to say "I'm always wrong" and "I hate myself." The two workshop leaders didn't blink an eye. They probably knew him and it was his usual shtick.

During a break, he leaned outside against the pole that held the basketball net. Grass grew through cracks on the court. I walked over. "You don't really hate yourself?"

He was startled. He thought an instant. "I guess I do."

"I don't believe it. You drive every day two hours from Portland to come here and two hours home. It means you want something."

In late afternoon the group went to a bar and shared a pitcher of beer. I nursed a sparkling water and positioned myself in the booth next to the depressed young man. "What do you do in the city?"

"I go to college." He paused. "A small, private Christian school."

I almost spit out my drink. "You feel comfortable there?"

"They all hate me." He reached out for a napkin with his right arm. The inside had a tattoo that said VOMIT. DEATH was another, written in Sanskrit. "It's a long story," he said, with the smallest curve up at the corner of his lips.

The piece he'd read in class that morning was about a mother's death. The son mixed her ashes in Evening in Paris perfume, then rubbed them into her sexy dresses and gave them away to the Salvation Army.

That evening Eddie and I charged into the freezing ocean over our heads. Rob panicked; what if we had heart attacks? I made a face at him, but he was serious.

As we were toweling off, I told him and Eddie what had been building in me all day. "I'm quitting," I said. "I'm not going back. I can't stand it. I don't belong. I'm done. I came to study with Spanbauer and he's not showing."

Rob and Eddie were stunned, and then agreed. "You're doing the right thing." They envied me, but they couldn't abandon the other students. We agreed that we would hang out at lunch breaks and in the evenings.

But back at the hotel the next morning while my friends were in class, I didn't know what to do with myself. I felt displaced, out of sorts in this resort town. I was on my own now to burn in hell.

The night before, I'd dreamed about my old Zen teacher. He'd been dead for fifteen years, and suddenly he came back in full force, beautiful with his bald head. He would not look directly at me, still mad from what I had written about him in my last book.

Then, in the dream, Carol Reisen, my old college pal, called to tell me our English teacher Mr. Crane had just come back from the dead too. He was the most boring teacher I'd ever had.

The last night, Tom had a party for the group. I went along with Rob and Eddie. Tom came alive at that party. He and I did the Lindy Hop together. He twirled me around double time. After the first dance, he took off his sweatshirt and I peeled off my cardigan. We meant business. The Rolling Stones came on. We screamed the words for "Jumpin' Jack Flash." Eddie leaped up, howling and stomping. He'd made it through his five-comments-a-day requirement. Now everything he saw and felt could be expressed through his body.

"Hey, wait a minute!" Tom yelled and ran over to a trunk. He pulled out spike-heeled pink satin slippers trimmed with feathers, flung off his shoes and slipped them on. He danced, kicking up his legs. He bent down and pulled up his jeans to where they stopped below the knees. Eddie followed, showing his hairy legs and brown oxfords.

Tom's boyfriend, Sage, changed the tape to Motown. Sweat poured off Tom's forehead. We fell to the couch after that second cut.

The next morning I finally had time alone with Tom. We were face-to-face early Saturday across a small square table. He wore a white T-shirt with an unbuttoned white tailored long-sleeve shirt over it. A thick gray moustache, curly gray hair, and a big nose. He was handsome, compelling. He wanted three eggs over easy and a side of ham. The waitress told him they didn't make over easy eggs here. He settled for scrambled.

What was it I wanted from Tom? He'd written his books; I'd written mine. We'd both been hippies. Almost sixty now, he told me that six years ago he'd broken up an eleven-year relationship, come down with full-blown AIDS, and lay alone in a hospital bed, where he almost died.

As a kid, close to open fields and distant mountains, isolated in a Mormon town right next to the Cheyenne/Shoshone reservation, he watched the unrelenting drinking of his family. "I've said that it was contracting HIV that saved me. I had to clean up my act, sleep at night, stop smoking. No more chugging beer. Otherwise, I would have gone the way of my people—stone-cold forever drunk—and soon dead."

Tom looked at me as he talked, his hands on the edge of the table. At one point he took off his long-sleeved shirt, revealing lean, knotted arm muscles built over years of baling hay at the farm. His strength was limited now. The disease had eaten away at him.

Leaning forward, I suddenly blurted out, "Tom, how come you never showed in class?"

He looked down and then up at me. "Can I tell you the truth?"

I nodded.

"My longtime students and I were having a hard time. And the fact that you were coming—a well-known writer—made things even worse. We thought of this plan—my students would teach the class and I would give individual conferences. Then we wouldn't have to teach together."

Tom went back to his cabin to get one of my books for me to sign. As I waited for him, a newcomer joined a group of people at the next table. "How's Ellen?" they greeted him.

"She's walking with the Word."

This is a friendly born-again place, I thought. *I'm walking with the word too. I've filled notebooks with it.*

Tom returned and handed me a book. I couldn't think of anything to write. *A pleasure to meet you* came to mind. That's all I can think of? I jotted down the platitude and signed my name.

We hugged good-bye in the street outside the café.

Eddie left early the next morning on the airport shuttle.

The following week, Rob and I wrote each day at the café across from our hotel. One morning at 7:00 he was right in front of me in line. He ordered coffee. The young girl behind the counter handed Rob a brown paper cup and he filled it with dark roast from a close-by thermos. I ordered a hot chocolate. This took longer. They steamed milk and ladled out cocoa. She asked my name to call it out when it was ready. I said, "Jane."

Rob's head swung around, but he took the leap and understood that a one-syllable name was easier than three. He nodded his head.

I went to a square table by the window, and he retreated to his by the wall. I immediately became absorbed, my hand moving fast. I had already filled three pages when the hot chocolate was shoved onto the table.

"It's okay, Jane, to use an alias. Only remember it when they call it out—over and over." Rob was standing above me, his hand on the cup.

"Oh, yeah, good idea." We allowed ourselves one moment of laughter—then back to our notebooks.

Later I called out to him across the crowded café, "Give me another word for 'response.'"

Hardly looking up from his page, he yelled out, "Retort, rebuttal, reply." Rob was my very own *Synonym Finder*.

At noon I crossed the street. I'd put in four and a half hours. That was plenty. I thought of the phrase "the loneliness of the long-distance runner."

I drove to Oswald West State Park and parked. I planned to hike up Neahkahnie, but it was not clear from the directions a friend had written down whether it was a two-and-a-half-mile trek till I got to the actual mountain, or if I was even in the right place to begin. But I didn't worry too much because I saw a trail and my legs were hungry to move.

I entered the dark woods, the soft path piled with russet needles, old-growth spruce looming above. Ferns filled the ground; moss grew on rocks and hung from trees. The earth was not bare and dirt was not visible anywhere. So different from my home state.

I came to a swinging bridge over a fast stream and did not hesitate. I felt like Tarzan—no, like Jane. Remember: Jane. I moved fast.

Why hadn't anyone told me about the Oregon coast? Easily as beautiful as Big Sur but so much less inhabited. No one was on the trail. After living at seven thousand feet for the last thirty years, sea level was a breeze for my robust lungs. Even a steep incline was easy.

The woods opened into a tangled trail rolling among abundant vines of near-ripe blackberries and pale raspberries. Over to the west was the Pacific, flat out between two cliffs. I was delighted in being half lost and half wandering.

I had written intensely all that morning, leaning over the notebook, deep in relation with my mind. A run to the bathroom was the only interruption to my concentration. This state of mind carried me out into the woods.

At first I turned my attention to the cool damp feeling of my skin, the sensation of my eyes adjusting to dark shadows, the blistering blue of the sky when I leaned my head far back to look beyond the stabbing spruce heights. Then, out of the corner of my right eye, almost like glimpsing a butterfly, something beckons. Once, twice, I let go.

I don't know how to say this—I give way to no thought at all, none arising and none passing away, to no perception, no smell or feeling, not even sound. I disappear. Sure, I continue with one foot in front of the other, but no coagulation of attributes named Natalie exists. If someone walked by, the person would see this woman in black cotton pants, white sneakers, a black V-neck T-shirt with the arms of a red sweatshirt tied around her waist. But inside there is no one. The reign of myself simply stops existing, dropping away.

I go on up the mountain and I come down the mountain and I walk to the sea. When I sit on a bench, sound enters me again. I hear the crash of waves. Filled with a knowledge that I will not last forever, a great impersonal sadness rolls through me.

I don't want to die. This is what I should have told Tom. But death will find me even if I don't have AIDS. Then this single thought: *Give everything while you can.*

9

Rain and the Temple

When I studied with Katagiri Roshi in Minneapolis, I never thought of going to Japan. I had my own little Japan with him. But when he died, I had a great desire to go. I wanted to see where he came from and the country that produced him—and that produced the Japanese Zen I was studying. I had a heart-to-heart connection with him, and that personal connection was really what carried me.

So I wanted to go to Japan, but I was scared. I had bought airplane tickets twice in the eight years since he died and then forfeited them.

But this time I decided I had to go. My partner, Michèle, agreed to come with me.

Right before we went, I visited Katagiri Roshi's wife, Tomoe, in Minnesota. I asked her for exact directions to his old temple. When his teacher died, it had become his temple. No one since had been abbot there. When I studied with Roshi, he'd told stories about it all the time. Only he and his teacher practiced in this temple.

Tomoe gave me directions, and this is how precise she was:

she not only told me where to get the bus after I took the train, but she opened up a photo album and showed me photos of the train station, the bus stop where I should get off, the spot where I should turn at the corner. And I thought, *Oh, Tomoe, I can find it.*

We arrive in Japan on a Thursday and go to Kyoto. The following Thursday morning I get up my courage to go out into the country. It is pouring rain. Pouring may be no big deal to someone who lives in San Francisco, but I live in New Mexico, where rain is an auspicious event. The rain in Kyoto scares me—it's flooding the streets. I think, *Should I go today?* And then I think, *Well, I planned to; okay, I'll go.* Michèle and I wear our green slickers. The Japanese only carry umbrellas, and they think it's very American and cloddish to wear these big plastic things on public transportation, where you have to sit all wet next to someone else.

We travel first on the subway, climbing four deep flights down. We take the subway to the train station, where we will catch the train to a town called Tsuruga. It's going to leave at 9:31, which in Japan means it leaves at exactly 9:31. This is really the only way we know that it's the right train. It shows up at 9:31 and we jump on.

I ask people sitting in their seats with newspapers and box lunches of pickles, rice, sushi, and seaweed on their laps, "Tsuruga? Tsuruga?" "Hai." Yes, we're on the right train, and it is pouring hard and the clouds are dark gray.

The train ride is an hour and ten minutes. We get off in a little town. We go to the small tourist station, but they don't speak a drop of English and I don't speak a speck of Japanese. I have the name for the next destination. I say, "Kitada?" "Kitada," they say, nodding. I want to ask, "Bus Two? Three? Where?" I hold up fingers. They point to two. It's bus two, leaving at 12:25. They write down "Kitada" in kanji on a slip of paper for us, so we can match it with the sign on the front of the bus.

We find the bus, but it's only 11:25. We have an hour to walk around.

Usually in the United States I don't eat lunch at the Greyhound bus station. But when I'm in other countries, I'm suddenly wide open, and we're hungry. We go into a tiny—I mean one small table width—restaurant. The waiter stands by us, pen poised to take our order. We point to something on the menu—not knowing what it is. The waiter speaks quickly with hands jerking and we nod and say, "Hai! Hai!" He shakes his head and goes into the back room.

A few other people are being served noodles, vegetables, and pieces of white fish. We aren't served, and the time goes by. I whisper to Michèle, "I think he was trying to tell us something important and we didn't get it." We have fifteen minutes until the bus leaves.

I screw up my courage, run into the kitchen, point to my watch, and hold up my hand. I flash five fingers three times—fifteen minutes till the bus leaves—but what my motions mean to the cook I have no idea.

I go back to my seat, and Michèle says, "So it's going to come?" I say, "Oh, yeah; he understood."

Ten minutes before the bus leaves, the waiter places an omelet before us. We're thrilled it isn't octopus. We eat it up quickly and run to the bus. I ask the bus driver: "Kitada?" He nods. "Kitada." Again I say "Kitada?" "Kitada."

We sit down, hoping someone will motion when we reach Kitada or that I'll recognize the bus stop from Tomoe's photo in the album.

People on the bus are staring at us—we are giants in green

slickers with no umbrellas. And it is still pouring out, the kind of rain that hits and bounces.

The bus moves through the wet countryside, and the road becomes narrow. People in the bus continue to gawk at us. Several times I run up to the bus driver and ask, "Kitada?" He nods. Finally everyone on the bus knows, so when we get there they yell in unison, "Kitada!"

We stumble out into the rain. The bus takes off, and we're left on the edge of the road next to a Japanese version of a 7-Eleven and a car repair shop.

Then we see a road. We begin walking down it. As soon as the road curves, we're in the Japanese countryside of rice fields, reeds, and ponds. In the distance we can see a village. No shops or bakeries, just little houses and farmed fields. It's beautiful through the slate-gray rain.

A heavy, powerful bird swoops down in front of us— feathered something like an owl but the royal size of an eagle. I say to Michèle, "What kind of bird is that?" It's the only bird out because it's raining so hard.

We trudge into the little town, where all shutters on houses are closed. The intricate flower pots drip with rain. Over a hill I see the Sea of Japan. I remembered Tomoe saying there was a sea. And so we keep going, and finally there is a marker in kanji.

I take a chance. "This is it," I say, hoping I recall it from one of Tomoe's photos. Behind it we see a mud path—the old entry-way, Tomoe told me. We both hesitate. Michèle says, "Let's follow it," and we step off the pavement. The earth is soggy, and we squish with each footstep.

In the distance I see a red-tiled roof—I know it is Taizoin Temple. There's one person in a paddy field in the rain, working with a hoe. He sees us walk by, and he turns. I wave, and he nods. Other big white people have come over time to visit Roshi's ashes.

The temple is deserted; there's no one to practice here anymore, since Roshi left for America more than thirty years earlier. The little village takes care of it. They open it for burials.

I see a little cemetery and say to Michèle, "Can I go by myself? I'll meet you."

It is an ancient cemetery with stone buddhas, tombstones, and decorative rocks. It is wonderful.

Then I panic. What if I don't find his tombstone? I walk around lots of old stones. Then, in the distance, I see a clutter of rounded tops. I know the rounded part signifies the marker of the teacher lineage for that temple.

I hurry over. At the very end is a newer tombstone. I know it is Roshi's. It is still pouring, but I push off my hood and throw off my slicker. I prostrate myself three times on the wet earth and then kneel in front of his stone. Pushing the dripping hair from my face, rain running down my cheeks, I speak to my old teacher. "I'm here. It took me a while, but I made it." I cannot say how good I feel to finally be there near some of his ashes.

I look around. Two rhododendron, a few trees I cannot name, but I can see them even now—dark green, tall, with drooping needles—a camellia bush, rice paddies, the Japan Sea, and the village. For years Roshi told me about this place. It was just him and his teacher practicing together. As a young monk, he thought that it was silly to get up in the morning. But his teacher kept a schedule, got up at five, sat zazen, made breakfast, and then he'd go and shake Katagiri. "C'mon, it's time to eat." And Katagiri would say, "Oh, I'll just sleep late." And his teacher would say, "It's good to follow the schedule, even if no one else is here."

Every few days they'd walk into town to formally ask the villagers for food with their begging bowls. And every time it was just the two of them, the teacher in front and the student behind.

When the student decided to come to America, he told his teacher. His teacher didn't discourage him, but Roshi told us, "When we walked into town, I could tell from his back that he felt lonely."

I remember the two of them as I sit in the rain in the cemetery. I make a vow to him, and I pick up a single black stone and put it in my pocket.

I go over to the temple. I was told it was locked, but Michèle finds a way to unlock it. We take our shoes off and go in.

It is a really old temple with a brick oven for a stove. We slide open paper walls, discovering spaces with tatamis on the floor.

The final place we find is a formal meditation hall with a large altar and a faded picture across the room. It must be Katagiri's teacher. A little photo is tucked into the bottom of the frame, very faded. I step closer. I can make out Roshi's profile. He must have sent it from America.

I stand in front of it a long time, as the rain thunders down on the roof.

When we leave, walking down the road, facing the Japan Sea, I know this is the path he took into the village.

Suddenly that brown bird swoops down in front of me and flies right back to the eaves of the temple. I follow him with my eyes and turn. I watch him open and close his wings as he clutches the edge of the roof with his claws. I swallow, lift my hand, wave good-bye, and keep walking.

Zigzagging

Zen is just zen
You can't ask sugar to give you protein
or a refrigerator to be a dog

Everything has its place

In a split second
my teacher died and
and I was left standing

10

Dog-Bite Enlightenment

There is a Zen story about an old monk who became disgusted after practicing for more than forty years in a monastery—*I'm getting nowhere,* he thought—and decided to leave. As he walked down the path to the gate, with his few belongings on his back, he noticed that the walkway looked a bit messy. He picked up a rake to smooth it out. As he raked the dirt, one pebble flew out, hit some standing bamboo nearby, and made a sharp *thwack.* The instant the monk heard that sound, he became enlightened.

I have been having terrible trouble this summer with my house out on the mesa. First it was the mice. Every day I caught three in my Havahart mousetrap. This went on for a month. At the end of August, teaching a two-week writing workshop at the Mabel Dodge Lujan House in Taos, I came into class and explained why I was late:

"As I was leaving the house, I heard the trap snap closed again. I thought, *That poor mouse will have to be in it all day. I better take her out now.* So I put down my car keys and my books, walked her down the long drive, crossed the road, aimed her at Michael's house, and let her go."

Each morning the class wanted to know how many were caught. I told them I was getting the funny feeling I was catching the same ones over and over. Kate Green, who was teaching with me, said, "Well, you put out a meal for them each night. Why wouldn't they return?" It was true—the night before I couldn't find anything else in my refrigerator, so I set out gourmet almond butter for them.

One morning, before I left to teach, the phone rang. "Eddie, I could swear the same mice are in the traps every morning."

"Nat, didn't you ever hear Mary's story? She was married to a man who had a cabin on an island in Rainy Lake, in northern Minnesota. He'd catch mice and take them in his canoe and let them off on another island. He'd say to Mary, 'I could swear they're coming back.' So he started to paint their toes with different colors of nail polish. Sure enough, when he caught mice again, they had polish on."

I drove across the mesa to class that morning thinking *D-Con, the poison that mice munch and then run from the house in search of water.* Last night, I saw four mice whiz across my living room as I read a book. It seemed to me they were almost frolicking, content from being well fed. I grew increasingly paranoid—I thought every shadow was another one. I read little that night. *D-Con,* I thought, and cackled as I turned my car toward Taos at the blinking light. I was tired of being the bodhisattva of mice.

On the way home from class, I stopped at Smith's and bought new and improved d-Con—two packages. I placed a box under the kitchen sink and another in the bathroom, where the mice had been feasting. I lay awake, thinking I heard them crunching on the poison, imagining I saw their small white ghosts arising right outside my bedroom window. I felt terrible and guilty. I finally dozed off at 3:00 A.M.

I woke up at four to a long animal screech. I was certain it was the mice dying. Then I was sure it was a cat who caught a poisoned mouse and he too was dying. I'd moved up the animal chain. I was ruining the entire neighborhood.

That morning when I woke up, there were no mouse turds. I looked gingerly around the house. No mice had dived into the toilet bowl, desperate for water. *Okay, I had one sleepless night,* I thought. I'd be okay.

Two days later, I took a bath—finally, my new well was working, though the water was still a bit muddy. I thought I smelled something burning. Kate was over; she was reading me some of her new poems as I lounged in the brown water.

"Go check the barbecue. Maybe it's something out there."

She came back. "Nope, everything's fine."

"I still smell it. Check the kitchen."

"Oh, my God," she shrieked. "Nat, the house is on fire. The water heater—it's in flames."

By the time I slid, wet, across the tiles, Kate had thrown water and put out the fire.

I stood there in a towel, looking at the smoldering remains of my Aquavac on-demand water heater.

On Tuesday the plumber came to replace it. I went over everything with him. When he left, I sighed. "Now I have everything. The heater's replaced. My well runs, and the mice are gone."

Twenty minutes later, as I spoke on the phone to a friend in Santa Fe, my telephone line went dead.

I knew I was going crazy as I drove across the mesa to teach my afternoon class. I passed my plumber, who had gotten a tire blowout after he left my house. I waved, asked him if there was anything I could do, and then kept going.

I parked at the post office. I thought I'd walk slowly across Kit Carson Park to the class. I needed to gather my wits. *Nat*, I kept saying to myself, *breathe. These things happen.*

I walked into the classroom. I told the students about the phone going dead. Then I told them about the old monk who became fully enlightened when a stone hit some bamboo.

Then I paused for a brief moment. I held up my hands. "What a fool I've been. That phone going dead! There was my chance! I could have turned everything around—that was it—in the face of distress, I could have become totally enlightened. Oh, my God, what a jerk I am!"

A student raised her hand. "Why don't you become enlightened now?"

"No, that was my moment! You can't do it later. I missed my moment."

But I think I did become enlightened for a while, once. I was quick enough, alert—no, that wasn't it. I was big; I wasn't myself. My cells had been tossed up inside my skull and fell down in another pattern. I saw things from a different angle, outside myself, my needs, my desires.

I was in southern France with Thich Nhat Hanh for three weeks in June, two years after my first retreat with him. I was forty-four years old. Each morning, Thay (Vietnamese for "teacher") lectured for three hours. I came early to the zendo and sat right in front of him. I was ready to have the teachings poured into me. He talked about the *Diamond, Lotus,* and *Avatamsaka Sutras.* Halfway into each morning, he switched the subject and told us another episode of when he fell in love as a young twenty-four-year-old monk with a twenty-year-old nun.

He said it was an accident—he was a monk; she was a nun. It was not supposed to happen. "Falling in love is an accident," he said. "Think about it: the expression *falling;* you trip into it." Because he did not act upon it in a romantic way, as we normally do, he examined these strong feelings with mindfulness, and forty years later, he shared the benefit of that with us. He was teaching the nature of love, of how to love well.

I flip through my notebook now and see the notes I took then. They seem to glimmer off the page: "Your first love has no beginning or end. Your first love is not your first love, and it is not your last. It is just love. It is one with everything."

"The present moment is the only moment available to us, and it is the door to all moments."

"When we practice mindfulness, we emit light. We create more time and space."

"The miracle is to walk on the earth."

"No coming. No going. Everything is pretending to be born and to die. That is a lie."

"This self has no self."

"A king once asked, 'Is there anything, any attachment, that will not cause suffering, anxiety, grief?' 'No, Lord,' said the Buddha."

"It is okay to suffer in the process of love."

I heard these things during those three weeks, and they poured into me. I received them, knew them to be true. I didn't try to understand them, figure them out with my logical mind. I walked differently on the earth because of them, and it continued after I left the retreat. Out in ordinary life, I felt a tenderness toward sidewalks; loved the tall sycamores lining Cours Mirabeau in Aix-en-Provence, where I went after the retreat; ate slices of pizza I bought in the streets as if they were part of the Last Supper.

Then, on July 8, two weeks out of Plum Village, I was bitten in the back of my right leg, above the ankle, by a trained guard dog who had been hiding when I walked up to a private house, thinking it was a café. My friends and I had wandered off from each other—we were in Saint-Rémy, near the monastery where Van Gogh had committed himself for a year. No little teeth indenting my skin—there was a chunk, a big one, hanging out of my leg. I didn't know this until I was halfway over the hill, moving fast through the woods, toward the monastery, the place I was meeting my friends. I stopped, turned my head, lifted the pale-green cotton pant leg. *Oh, my God! It can't be as awful as that or I couldn't be walking.* I dropped my pant leg and got to the monastery office, banged on the door, yelling. There was a rush of women inside; the door opened.

"Un chien!" I yelled, and made the motion with my hands together, opening and closing, like a crocodile's jaw (I didn't know the French word for *bite*). "Ma jambe." I pointed to my pant leg. I didn't lift it though. I didn't want these nurses and nuns to collapse in a dead faint.

"Un grand chien?" they asked.

"Non, une grande bouche." I was in a panic. "Aidez-moi!"

They called an ambulance.

Now the remarkable thing: Not for a moment did I feel hatred for the dog. At the moment of our confrontation, I felt compassion for him. Thay had lectured us about "looking deeply." The dog had been trained to do what he was doing. This was no act of personal violence. This was the result of the lineage of private property, of ownership, of fear of loss of possessions. I do not mean to sound high-handed here, or even political—I just saw into the depth of the act, where and how it came about. The dog bit once—deftly, swiftly—and retreated. I fell on my left knee. He growled fiercely, as though to warn me, "Get out of my space." I crawled out of the range of his chain.

In the ambulance—it was an old car carrying me to the hospital in Avignon—I sat in the back, my leg up along the length of the seat. "Depechez-vous," I called to the driver. She lit a cigarette. We passed groves of bamboo and fruit trees. I had left a note at the monastery for my friends: *Meet me at the hospital.*

In the back of the car, I thought, *If Buddhism's gonna work, it's gonna work now. Breathing in*—I inhaled—*I know I am breathing in. Breathing out*—I exhaled—*I know I am breathing out.* I am always breathing in and out, but it is rare that I am aware of it. *Breathing in, I know I am breathing in.* Actually, I was delighted to be aware of my breath. It gave me something to do besides freak out about what had just happened to my leg.

We turned the corner into the hospital parking lot. I was put on a gurney and wheeled into a small room.

Two nurses lifted up my pant leg. "Oh, mon dieu." Their eyes wide, their hands thrown across their open mouths. They ran and got other nurses, orderlies. Everyone was emotional.

"Un grand chien?" was the only medical question that I was asked.

Breathing in—I was scared. Breathing out—I was afraid. High school French failed me. "Un docteur?" I moaned.

A man came in wearing a white T-shirt. He looked; he said, "It all right. It okay." He put his hand on my leg.

"Oui?"

"It okay." It was the only English anyone spoke in the whole hospital. He made the motion with his hand that he was going to have to sew.

I nodded yes, I understood.

He left.

I lay there, waiting.

I looked away as the doctor worked. A second felt like a year. He hummed a little. We were alone in the room. *Okay, Nat, what are you going to do now?* Breathing in and knowing it wasn't quite enough.

I was facing the wall. I began to sing a song I'd learned at the retreat. I sang it loud. The lines, "I'm as solid as a mountain, as firm as the earth," comforted me the most. I repeated them over and over and skipped the rest of the song. Was this possible? I was filled with joy. I felt such gratitude to be alive. The air shimmered. I wanted to turn to the doctor and touch him, thank him.

He was done. I turned. "Combien?" I asked. "How many?"

He made a face. "Beaucoup."

I held up ten fingers. "Non." He shook his head. He flashed twenty fingers. "Vingt soutures."

I nodded.

The nurse came in. She had given me a tetanus shot earlier. She showed me a card. I had to get another shot in a month. Another in a year.

My friends Rita and Phyllis came to the door. "I can leave," I said. We were so happy to see each other.

I sat in the backseat of our rented car.

"Let's sing," I said. All three of us had been to Plum Village. We drove through the countryside. "And I know there is space deep inside of me . . . I am free, I am free."

Rita was driving. "We should go back to the hotel. You're in shock."

"No, I want to go to these medieval towns I've been reading about," I insisted. I looked at the map. I wanted to live every moment now.

We drove down winding, narrow country dirt roads. "Pull over," I said.

We got out of the car and looked around. Fruit trees—three of them—in tall grass near vineyards. I walked over and looked up. Cherries, all ripe, many fallen to the ground. No farmer was going to gather this crop. I grabbed fistfuls, hobbled with my bandaged leg from clump to clump, my hands dripping red.

"Aren't you afraid a guard dog is going to come?" Rita called, standing by the car, snapping a picture of me.

"Nah, no dog wants to harm me. That was a Mu dog, a Zen dog, that bit me. He said, 'Wake up!'" I laughed. "Rita, these are *bing* cherries. Bing. Do you understand? They are my father's favorites. I always imagined they grew on vines, not trees." Phyllis stood under the tree too, grazing alongside me.

I filled a big bag full of them. Then we drove in the dusk past a faded *chocolat* sign overlooking a beautiful valley.

We were stopped in Cavaillon by truckers drinking wine out of bottles, their massive semis parked in the road—a blockade. They were demanding more lenient license laws. They let us pass. We drove on and on, the car carrying us back to Aix.

I loved the Hotel Splendide. I loved my room, with the window opening onto the orange tile roofs of the city. Just that morning I had lain there looking out, carefree, the swallows scissoring the morning sky. Both legs intact. Now the local anesthetic was wearing off. A dog had bitten my leg.

The next day I stayed in bed. Rita brought me quiche and purple flowers. Phyllis drew my portrait. I read *The Great Gatsby* in its entirety. I'd bought it two days earlier at an English-language bookstore. The cover photo was black-and-white, a sleek boulevard with a man and woman leaning against a thirties sedan. In a foreign country, I discovered the American classics again. I looked toward that continent where I was born and wondered, *Who am I, anyway? And what is the American dream?*

I finished the book and looked down at my leg, then at the water lily wall painting the owner of the hotel had done, and I knew I was in my own dream.

The next day Rita and I went to the emergency room of the Aix hospital. I needed to get my wound dressed, and no one at the other hospital spoke enough English to tell me what to do. We found a doctor there who spoke some English.

"It may become infected. Maybe okay. Maybe you need operation. They take skin from your hip"—he pointed to my hip—"and put on leg." He pointed to the dog bite.

Rita and I looked at each other. It wasn't going to heal in ten days, in time for me to fly to London? I was going to have to leave and return to the States.

A reality map spread out in front of me. Suddenly Rita and I were bewildered young girls together in a foreign country. She told me about her father's funeral in New York. "You know it's going to happen someday, but there you are picking out a coffin. Whose life is this, you think?"

I made reservations to get a flight the next day from Nice to Minneapolis—my close friend there is a doctor.

My plan to fly to London to meet my friend Henry and travel around Scotland was just an idea—even though I had made travel arrangements. It was a concept, a future moment. It did not exist, except in my head. In a moment your whole life can change. "It is not because of impermanence that we suffer but because of our ideas about permanence," Thich Nhat Hanh had told us.

I called Henry and told him I couldn't come, but I was not suffering. I miraculously was not holding on to any plans, and I did not know it was miraculous. I was living my life. I was in it in a way I'd never been in it before. It was burning pure white.

The plane had engine trouble near London, and we had to come down. I was taken in a wheelchair—my leg had become swollen—to a bus that drove us from Heathrow to Gatwick. I looked out at the green grass of England, at the sturdy homes. I had to board another plane, and we landed in New York too late to catch a plane to Minneapolis. There were long lines as Delta figured out hotel and plane reservations for all of us at Kennedy. I sat in another wheelchair. The porter went ahead of the line and got me new reservations. Then he told me I had to wait with the rest of the group for a bus to go to the Holiday Inn.

"Will the bus be outside?" I asked.

"I suppose so," he answered.

"Well, could you wheel this outside? I'll wait there. I need real air. I've been in planes and airports for nineteen hours."

He brought me to the front door and left me outside. The air was humid, the sky hazy. And past the hustle of taxis and sweaty people of every color and language, wearing shorts and thongs and baseball hats, greeting each other, grabbing arms and hands, was the full moon, like an ancient call, big and fat, out there in the dark.

The porter came back ten minutes later. "Wanna come back in? It's hot out here." He put his hand to his neck. "Air cool in there." He nodded toward the door.

"No, thanks," I said. "I'd like to sit here with the moon." He laughed, looked up at it, wiped his brow, and left.

I remained in my wheelchair, my right leg stretched out, my blue nylon suitcase hanging from one arm of the chair and my red nylon purse hanging from the other, until the bus came twenty minutes later.

In Minneapolis, my leg was a waiting game. Would the flap that they sewed back in France survive? I could walk or lie down, be straight, vertical or horizontal; but sitting cut off vital blood flow. I lay on my side in Carol's living room.

I'd met Carol ten years earlier in a Hebrew class when I still lived in the Twin Cities. After I left, we became traveling partners. Every two years or so, we would meet for a month in Czechoslovakia, Amsterdam, Portugal, Israel. Now I was back in Minneapolis with her.

Each night she patiently helped me with my dressing. After she went to sleep, I'd open the shade of my bedroom window and smell summer through the screen and see the moon reflected on the thin square of wires that kept out the flies. "The Midwest," I'd whisper, "the Midwest," and I'd feel the corn in distant fields turn out its seeds.

I sat in the suburbs of Minneapolis all day, alone, while Carol went to work. Sometimes I lay on her front lawn and looked up at the elms and maples. Big ones. I walked to the mailbox, down those asphalt streets, the early afternoon so still and empty. A man looked out his window, his lawn perfectly trimmed, his shutters white, his sprinkler poised for action. The sunlight waved the tree leaves in shadows across me. The mail was picked up at 2:15 every weekday, and on Saturdays pickup was at twelve. "Noon" was written on the inside lid of the blue metal mailbox.

I hobbled to the Lincoln Del each day—five blocks away— for matzo ball soup. On Wednesday they had a special: a bowl of soup and half a sandwich for $4.95. As I leaned my head over the steaming bowl, I noticed that the same old people were there every day. There was a retirement community four blocks away. A few days earlier, I was in France, land of Manet, Monet, Matisse, Picasso, Van Gogh, Cézanne. Now I was in the suburbs of the Midwest with old people, an ulcer on my leg, glad for my chicken soup. I remembered an old Jewish joke whose punch line was "I know where I *want* to go, but I don't know where I'm going."

I walked back to Carol's, looked for the mailman, did a few paintings the size of postcards. One was of a small dog with a large mouth. I wrote on it, "Un chien n'est pas grand, mais la bouche est grande." Another was of a traffic intersection with the signs saying SLOW and YIELD, ending at Heaven Café. In the foreground were three ducks and a green lawn, and it was raining on them. "Il pleut tres bien," I wrote below them.

Carol had a day off in the middle of the week. "Let's go to Lake Rebecca," I proposed.

"Nat, where's that?" she asked. She loved anything new.

I told her it was nearby. I would direct. She should just drive and not remember the directions. It was a secret place, I told her.

We put down the back of the passenger seat so I could remain horizontal and my foot wouldn't swell. As we rode through the green countryside, past fruit stands and gas stations, I told her, "You'll see, no one will be there. Minnesotans are chauvinistic about their state. Yes, there are good things here, but they miss what the *real* good things are. For twenty years Katagiri Roshi lived here in a little zendo on Lake Calhoun. Hardly anyone ever came! What they missed!"

I loved to carry on about Minnesotans. The people I loved and hated, how could they be so good? It drove me crazy when I lived here for six years. I always had the strange urge to take off my clothes and run down their streets screaming. But when I went away from them, moved to another state—where the license plates herald the Land of Enchantment—I missed the Minnesotans, their rootedness; their sincerity; their gentle, easy openness; their good old American virtues of truth, honesty, and justice that the rest of us have just about forgotten.

I went on to tell Carol about the bank in Owatonna, two

hours south. "Everyone thought I was nuts. 'A bank?' they'd ask. It was designed by Louis Sullivan. He called it a color form poem, and it's one of the most magnificent buildings I've ever seen. It has a beautiful mural of cows inside."

"Cows?" She laughed. Carol was brought up on a farm in North Dakota.

"Precisely," I said. "Cows. You midwesterners don't know what you've got."

We drove through the town of Maple Grove. I lifted my head from my horizontal position to look over the bottom edge of the window. This was the town Neil and I drove out to in order to get a special chocolate wedding cake for our marriage a zillion years ago. A woman baked them out here in her home. Six tiers, a plastic man and woman on top, yellow fringe hanging from each layer, the chocolate icing dark and laid on thick, packed with sugar to keep it stiff.

Carol parked the car. I was right. The park was empty. I slung her old blue bedsheet from the trunk over my shoulder, and we walked down the path that brought us to swans in a far-off pond, to an old white barn with a black roof, through prairie grass, past beehives standing in fields.

My pace slowed down more and more. Neil and I used to come here all the time and lie naked in the open fields. I remembered walking hand in hand, slightly bored, relaxed, no beginning or end to the afternoon. He would hum a tune, his thin, red, freckled hand in mine. Sometimes he would tell me a story about his grandmother Chloe, in Kankakee, Illinois. *I loved that man,* I thought. I loved him deep and long, and it would be forever, though we had divorced twelve years earlier. I felt sad and happy that we had known the kind of love we had together. Something pure in its innocence—the kind of innocence that eventually destroys itself.

Carol and I walked on and on in silence. The sky was a big gray, and a slow wind moved the tall grasses. I spread her bed-sheet on the ground and we lay down.

At the end of two weeks, I had my third visit with the plastic surgeon. I felt so confident that the flap had gotten enough blood and was healing that I told Carol I'd go to the doctor by myself. I'd see her after work.

I took a taxi to the medical building. Two weeks earlier, I knew nothing about dog bites. Now I thought I was an authority.

The nurse took off the bandage. I looked at it all the time now—when I first arrived in Minneapolis, I was afraid to look. The stitches were in the shape of a tongue, but larger—the size of a coffee mug. And just like Frankenstein, with his stitches accentuated across his face, those stitches that the French doctor had given me were visible. You could count each one and even see the knot where he ended. The thread was black. He'd had a regular sewing bee in the operating room.

I said to the doctor when he walked in, "It's my professional opinion that it's doing really well. Carol and I conferred. Her only concern is that the flap skin is a little yellow."

"Let's have a look." He bent over it. "*Hmmmm.*" He tapped and poked. "It's not making it. We'll have to cut it out."

Everything blurred. A nurse assisted him. It happened fast. The whole flap was cut out, all that the French doctor had sewn back in. It didn't survive. "You'd better look," the doctor said. "You are going to have to dress it every day." I told the doctor I didn't want a graft from my hip. I'd forget being Miss America and live with the big scar after the gash healed.

"No, I can't dress it." I had my head turned to the wall. "I just can't look. I'll do it some other time. Carol will look at it."

"It would be better to look at it now, while I'm here."

I heaved my head around. "Oh, my God!"

The plastic surgeon actually held me. I felt his comfort flow into me. He understood my fear. He had a tenderness that amazed me. Carol had told me that he had fought cancer and survived.

I went back to Carol's in a cab. She was home. All I said to her was, "Please take me for a malt."

We sat outside on the patio of an ice-cream parlor near Lake Harriet. I spooned the chocolate malt into my mouth. I began to sob. I fell over the table and cried and cried.

This was another miracle. I'd been living right there with everything in front of my face, moment by moment, since I had been bitten by the dog in France. But now, who was I crying for over my malt? Not for me, though I was scared. Inside me, like a column of white light, I felt overwhelming gratitude and tenderness for that doctor. I could walk out of his office with a bad leg. There wasn't a question of life and death.

I also felt the life of my teacher, Katagiri Roshi, who had gone in and out of the hospital right across from the medical building I had just been in. Chemotherapy treatments, radiation, infection. Life and death. Life and death. I felt him in his car after a treatment, exhausted, dauntless, a Zen student driving him back through the winter streets of Minneapolis to his apartment above the zendo, his wife of thirty years in the backseat next to him. She told me once that for that whole year, they were never outside. In hospitals, in cars, in beds, in bedrooms, away from harsh weather, drafts, breezes.

When I quieted down, Carol asked quietly, "How are you doing?"

"Roshi didn't make it." I pushed the malt away from me. "I am so lucky to be alive."

· · ·

The Saturday before I left Minnesota, Carol and I drove down to the Zen land on the bluffs of the Mississippi near New Albin, Iowa. A portion of Katagiri Roshi's ashes were there. We arrived at midday, the sun hot, the air thick and humid—it had rained earlier that day. I told Carol I needed to go up there alone, and I climbed the high hill where his monument was. I went slow, my right leg bandaged, the grass tall, thigh high.

There is a ceremony you're supposed to do when you visit the memorial—with water and thick scrub brushes, incense and offerings. You are supposed to carry all of this up. I carried it all maybe a quarter of the way; then it became too hard. I dropped the buckets of water, let go of everything else, and hobbled up the rest of the way empty-handed. I collapsed on the smooth granite on which his name was carved.

I looked out over the valley. The spruce trees we had planted for future generations ten years ago, as soon as we bought the land, were now way above my head. I could see the brown tar paper roof of the zendo and the porch around it, the bell, the kitchen beyond it, the slow Winnebago Creek, the supply room, Roshi's cabin.

I sat on the memorial of my great dead teacher, looked out on the great world.

Then I turned to him. "Roshi, you know I'm a fuckup." Then I began to laugh. What a terrible and devoted Zen student I had been. He knew all about me. I'd been his student for twelve years. "Sorry, I don't have the incense and the scrub brushes." I laughed some more and felt a bitterness too. He wasn't in the flesh to laugh with me.

Then I just sat there for a while. I began to get up, and then I sat down again. "Roshi, what do you think about love?" I asked.

A slow joy, a trickle of heat entered my chest. "To love is a good thing," I heard him once say.

I began my slow walk down the hill. A moment later I heard a terrible snorting. I flung my head around—a deer! A beautiful chestnut-colored deer leaped out from behind Roshi's hill. I would never have seen her if she hadn't snorted. She ran like a dancer, all four hooves in the air, and then she disappeared into the forest.

I whistled the rest of the way down the hill and picked up the buckets and brushes near the bottom.

II

Iowa

The plane drops down into Cedar Rapids and the snow is falling thick and at an angle. The flight attendant announces it is eighteen degrees. Monday, February 11. The next day my new book *Old Friend from Far Away* will be on sale and I will read at the independent Prairie Lights bookstore. The publisher has forgotten to assign an escort or tell me how to get from the airport to the Sheraton in Iowa City, thirty miles away.

I explain this to the woman sitting next to me. She has high heels and thick legs, is wearing nylons and a black skirt. She tells me that she and her husband are driving to the Quad Cities, and they can drop me off. Her big husband in the next seat says nothing.

"If you don't mind," I say, looking straight at him. He looks ahead.

The alternative is to grab a shuttle, which I learn in the terminal won't be running for an hour. There's a blizzard outside.

I ask the woman to watch my bag as I go out to a yellow cab.

"Seventy-five dollars," he tells me. I look in the cab at his long stringy hair and very big belly. "Nope, too much," I say, and go back through the electric door.

"I'll get the car," the thick-legged woman says, and walks off into the blizzard in her heels.

Her husband is in khakis and a straw hat. They have just returned from Mexico, and he is not ready to bundle up.

We wait a long time. "I think she can't get the car started," he says.

I see another yellow cab, grab my suitcase, and take my chance. "Iowa City?" I hop in with a college girl and we split the fare.

What am I doing here in the middle of winter?

As we pull onto the highway, I remember: the Midwest.

The tires are bald, but the driver is fearless. He says he knows snow, and I believe him. The white of the sky reaches down to the white of the land, broken on the horizon here and there by a few bare trees. I can't help it—I love this place. Barren and beautiful.

The cab drives down a rutted alley and swings in front of my hotel. The bellboy in a navy-blue overcoat that's way too big for him steps out to take my luggage.

I move quickly into the revolving door, then stop. I swivel my head. "How old are you?"

"I'm older than I look—twenty-two."

"You can vote?"

Everything is distilled down to that these days. Obama had won this state in the primaries a few weeks earlier. I watch political coverage on television now, want a glance of Hillary's daughter, of Barack's wife, Michelle. "So who'd you pick?" It's not American to ask, I know. Voting should be a private thing.

"I didn't."

"Please," I say. "You don't want a Republican again?"

He's not sure; I can see it in his face. Then he takes a leap. "Oh, no, ma'am."

"Promise me you'll vote on election day."

He promises. I give him a dollar for bringing up my bags—I should have given him two. He tells me there is an escape map behind the door in case of fire and points to a thermostat across from the bathroom.

"You promised," I remind him. He backs out the door.

From my fifth-floor window I can see all of downtown: the green walking bridge; the clock tower with the wrong time; the two bank clocks, a half hour apart; the thickened steam filling the air from the heat exchangers on the roofs; the shoveled paths on the sidewalk; the brick buildings. A café across the street. I can walk everywhere if I don't mind the weather.

A block away a clutch of pedestrians crosses the street together. A light must have changed.

The people who live here were born here. Not everyone, but many. Who else would live here? Refugees from Vietnam and Somalia filled Minneapolis in the last years I was there. From jungles to glaciers. That's painful. I'd rather it be the other way around. But Minnesotans like their cold and their snow.

The Midwest was good to me. I learned to be a writer there, where writers were organized—classes, jobs, grants, fellowships, bookstores, publishing. When I left for the wilderness of New Mexico, the only thing that made me a writer was the brute force of my pen on paper. No comfortable café to chat about the new book or magazine or the grant to apply for. I either reached a New York publisher or moved into oblivion. I was lucky, and my first book met America at a pivotal place. It was the years in the Heartland that made me ready, gave me the foundation. But I couldn't live there forever. I didn't belong. People there made their friends in grammar school.

I called the front desk. "It's awfully dry here and I'm fighting a virus. Do you have a humidifier?"

No, they didn't. The young girl is sorry.

Forty-five minutes later the phone rings simultaneously with a knock at the door. "Humidifier," a man calls from the hall, while from the receiver a voice says, "We found it in the basement."

They'd been looking all this time? Only in the Midwest.

The next morning I see the bellhop in the lobby. "Today they are competing in Maryland, Virginia, and DC. Your job is to stay abreast of the count and keep me informed."

He is delighted and salutes me.

I go out into the frigid air, my head wrapped in a wool shawl. The hairs in my nostrils freeze. The first two women's shops I pass display mannequins in bareback sleeveless dresses and shorts. I enter the third shop. "What's with the bathing suits?"

"It's our spring selection."

"You're kidding. Isn't it a little early?" It is six below outside and no one is walking slow.

The salesgirl shrugs her shoulders.

I stop to check my e-mail at a coffee shop. My college friend Carol's mother had a stroke and will likely die within a week. I remember her clearly. She swam laps, wore short hair, and drove a fast car.

My mother had died six weeks earlier, on December 24. I can't wrap my mind around her death. It follows me like a ghost. But every time I turn around to look at it, it vanishes. I have a lot of crying to do, but it isn't coming. Something is over, but I don't yet know what it is.

My book is out in bookstores today. The one I wrote the year I broke up an eleven-year relationship.

I'm afraid that if I think too much about my mother, I'll drop this book tour and fly to Florida, go to the small house she lived in alone for the last eight years after my father died. The one with her yellow blouses still hanging and her bras in the top drawer and her hearing aid on the snack table by the big blue chair. Afraid I'd move in there and try to figure out what my life was all about, free of her barbs and criticism.

Instead, I'm back in the Midwest. The Mississippi, the bluffs, the stands of trees, white clapboard houses. I want to belong somewhere. The Midwest gives you that illusion of home, especially when you're lost and looking in the wrong places.

When I return to the hotel, the bellboy pounces on me. "Clinton's ahead in Maryland." He gives me the numbers.

"Check again soon. Not for long."

I didn't give a damn if the youth were inspired by Obama. I wanted my generation to have one more chance to do right. When it was my turn to vote in the primary, I went for Obama. It felt right—in the spirit of my generation. A week later the ballots in New Mexico were still being counted. How embarrassing. What a backward state. Maybe I should move to Iowa.

Despite the blizzard, a hundred people come to my reading. I'm going to be interviewed on the radio for an hour in front of the audience. Next week it will be broadcast all over the state.

From the time the announcer introduces me, I can't shut up. My whole heart is in this book. I want everyone to know this— also that I will die someday, just like my mother, just like them, and that this book is the closest thing to being in the classroom with me. Someday I won't be around to stand in front and say, "Class, take out your notebooks and fast writing pens."

The people staring at me look awfully young. "How many of you are still in high school?" I keep asking. No one raises a hand.

"I'm teaching you what you should have learned in high school—how to trust your own mind, have confidence in your own experience—so you don't vote for the wrong person, like so many of us did last time."

I didn't care that it's not politically or socially correct to talk politics when I'm trying to sell memoir. We have to get out of Iraq. We have to close Guantanamo. I'm so ashamed of what our country has become. My grandparents, whom I loved, loved this country. I wanted to love it again too. "You should write so you know who you are and what you think. So you can stand up. 'Life, liberty, and the pursuit of happiness—and writing.'"

Some of my books sell out. That night I trade the bookstore the flower arrangement a kind friend sent to me at the bookstore for a calendar of Fallingwater, the Frank Lloyd Wright–designed house outside of Pittsburgh.

On the way back to the hotel I stop at a sandwich shop. Jim White, a poet I knew a long time ago, said that after a reading you have to either drink, eat, dance, or fuck.

When I enter the lobby later, the bellboy runs up to me. "The numbers have all changed. Barack won."

"Well, of course he did." I stop and point at him. "Now remember, you promised to vote. We need you."

"I will. I will."

A few minutes later I'm standing in my room, looking out the window. Already I'm beginning to love my country again. I envision a closed prison in Guantanamo, an Iraq at peace, a world where I belong. The snow outside continues to fall.

I'm too restless to stay in my room. I shoot up in the elevator to the ninth floor, where they have a free computer to do e-mail.

A young girl with an accent is at the terminal. I sit on the big leather lounge chair eating a slice of green melon they have left out for guests. It is good. I have another and then another. They are free. I eat them until I get a stomachache, and the computer is still occupied.

12

Writing as a Visual Art

A show of Richard Diebenkorn's work had been mounted at the Harwood Museum of Art, a fifteen-minute walk from where I was conducting a writing workshop with sixty students at the Mabel Dodge Luhan House in Taos, New Mexico. The Harwood used to be the town's library, where I taught English classes to my ratty high school students from the nearby hippie school in 1974. We would straggle down Randall Lane past the wild asparagus growing among the ditch weeds in March and huddle together in a circle on small wooden chairs trying to figure out similes for mountain and apple and horse.

The Harwood was also where I wrote the novel *Banana Rose*. I brought a lunch box each day for break under the elms out back, sitting on a wood bench overlooking the south of town. Soon after the novel was written, the Harwood became an art museum, and the town built a public library near the courthouse with funds from bond investments.

All of this was irrelevant to my workshop students from all over the country, who'd been writing full-out for three days. One student from Chicago wrote of working in the women's penitentiary and of a prisoner who had tried to shoot herself but missed and killed her son instead and was incarcerated for murder.

I closed my eyes after hearing her read. The inconceivable hell we human beings live with.

Another young woman began: "I'm wondering what my father's life was like living in Korea during the Korean War. He was seven years old in an orphanage. His job was to bury kids who died who were younger than him. He was given a single pair of shoes and three years later had that same pair, and I know at ten his feet were not the same size."

Again and again I encouraged: "Give us a picture. Don't keep your life private. Share it. Make it vivid." And they certainly did that. The course was entitled Living Color: Writing as a Visual Art.

How was I to seduce these writing students, so deep into words on the fourth day of class, over to visit this abstract art exhibit? I wanted to share this visual delight with the class.

I was proud of my small town of Taos for pulling this show together. The curators had worked diligently for four years. The University of New Mexico produced a coincident beautiful art book that cost fifty dollars. And after September 9 the show would travel to San Jose, California, and then to New York University in the Big Apple, the final nod on what's good.

Early in his career in the fifties, Diebenkorn, based in California, spent two years working on an MFA at the University of New Mexico in Albuquerque, using funds from the GI Bill. The Harwood gathered all the paintings he'd done during that period. They had to borrow work from Stanford University, the Norton Simon Museum, Oakland Museum, Oklahoma City, and private collections, including one oil, ink, and gouache from Milan, Italy. The stipulation of the insurance company that covered the paintings, worth easily up in the six figures, was that the Harwood had to provide a guard at the exhibit at all times.

I'd already made four visits to the show. On my last I sidled up to the guard on watch, a hefty local boy in uniform with a crew cut, and asked him what he thought of the paintings. "Well, I'm with them every day. At first I thought they were nothing. But they aren't nothing. They are something. Look at that black—I can see red and blue and pink in it now." He shook his head. "I won't forget this, I'll tell you. I'll remember it."

In an hour I needed to transport these students out of our classroom and out of the mind of writing to the silent mind of paint. What did Richard Diebenkorn have to do with them? I had to make it relevant. We planned to drive in a procession of twelve cars the less than a mile distance around the plaza, bearing right onto Ledoux Street.

I reached for something seemingly far away and reeled it in, hoping to give them an opening, an entrée to Richard Diebenkorn. I began my tale: "Two years ago I found myself living in Palo Alto for six months, not knowing anyone. I heard that a woman in town conducted a weekly writing group and they did the practice methods I taught.

"'Do you think I could come?' I humbly asked one of the group members on the phone.

"I received directions and in my great loneliness turned right, then left onto La Para to the home of Helen Bigelow, who was conducting these Thursday evenings for free.

"Six women, mostly in their sixties and early seventies, one, I think, in her eighties, sat in a circle. Helen's husband, Ed, who also wrote with them, pointed to a corner of the couch. I flopped down.

"Helen said 'Go' and everyone plunged into their notebooks.

"'Wait; for how long?' I beseeched them.

"'Don't worry about that.' Helen waved her hand. She looked vaguely familiar, but everyone was galloping along, so I dove in too. We wrote page after page. I kept looking up for some signal to stop. After about fifty minutes, with no sign from anyone, they began to wind down.

"I looked at Helen again. Was she that student from years ago?

"We went around the circle, reading aloud all the pages we'd written.

"Then the woman opposite me pulled out a joint from her bra, lit the tip, and passed it around. I was stunned—I hadn't smoked in years; when it came to me, I took two long draws and passed it on. Then I took another two on the second pass.

"Again Helen said 'Go.'

"Are you kidding? My brain was on the ceiling. Off everyone went with pens on paper.

"After we all wound down, we were beckoned to the dining room table for a dinner of salmon, salad, and bread. Every week Helen served a meal. This had been going on for how long? I tried to calculate the years since she might have studied with me, but at that moment I couldn't add or subtract.

"At 1:00 A.M. I drove the less-lonesome streets home, but not sure where the lane of traffic began or ended.

"These women were not part of the dot-com world of Silicon Valley (my partner, who was managing a start-up, was the reason I had moved there). They had deep roots in California and had known Ken Kesey, who had lived with a group of friends in small bungalows in the sixties on Perry Lane.

"I went to the group every week for a month," I told the class. "On the fifth visit Helen greeted me at the door.

"'I'd like to show you my oak tree,' she said, and we went to the rear of the yard.

"Our heads tilted back as we looked deep into the dark sky. The oak was massive, at least two hundred years old.

"'You know,' she said, 'you have been my teacher all of these twenty years since that one time I studied with you in the late eighties.'"

"'Let's have lunch,' I said.

"She suggested we meet the day after at a wonderful café on California Avenue.

"Lined on the counter was a chocolate soufflé, a peach kuchen, blueberry crisp, a high layer cake. We perused the menu and chatted. I was happy.

"'So what are you working on?' I asked.

"'A memoir about my father, who was a painter,' she flicked her eyes a moment from the menu.

"I was filled with hesitation. I could switch the subject or hear about what I presumed was her father's weekend watercolor hobby. I jumped in: 'So what kind of painting did your dad do?'

"'My father was David Park.' She looked straight at me with those blue eyes.

"'Your father is David Park? You're kidding.' David Park was a great painter.

"'Are you sure?' I stupidly asked.

"'Of course, I'm sure.' She laughed.

"I flashed on the walls of her living room. Some ordinary pictures, then over on the far wall was a large oil portrait of a woman, so strong, so powerful, I'd see it out of the corner of my eye and turn away—it made me nervous, like hanging an original Jackson Pollack in my family's split-level house—the contrast would make the house collapse.

"'That's your father's painting of the woman?'

"Helen nodded. 'It's of my mother, Lydia.'

"My mouth hung open. 'You knew Richard Diebenkorn? Wasn't he your father's student?'

"'Yes, and then they became close friends, along with Elmer Bischoff. I was twenty-seven, with three young girls, when David died. I remember so clearly going over with my mother to Dick and Phyllis's home. Over the fireplace was a new painting, still wet, by Dick. I stopped dead in my tracks. It was gorgeous. I told him so.

"'I want you to have it, Helen,' he said.

"'Oh, I can't.'

"'Please, I really want to give it to you.'

"'I kept refusing. Only later—when it was too late—did I realize he meant it. His best friend, his great colleague, had just died and he felt helpless. It was something he could do. He could give a painting to David's daughter.'

"David was an important, influential painter, one of the leading artists of the Bay Area Figurative movement, but he was not world famous. He was on his way, but he died too young, of cancer, at forty-nine."

The class was mesmerized. I decided to push further.

"A couple months ago I was in New York for a conference. On the one evening the Whitney was open late, I dashed uptown. Dusk settled over the city as I showed my ticket to the guard and moved over to the stairs. I can't remember what floor—maybe on the fourth or fifth—I headed for the permanent collection. I was hoping to get a gander at some Edward Hoppers, but I was seduced into the pleasure of seeing one painting after another by world-class mid-twentieth-century artists. After a while I stood in the doorway of a large room. A Willem de Kooning was across from me. A Joan Mitchell kitty-corner. And then I entered and turned around to my right. *Oh, my God. There it was.* One huge David Park took up the whole wall." I spread my arms wide to show the students.

"A man rowing away, one oar in the water, one out. From the man's back emanated a stark sadness and vibrancy all at the same time. In the foreground three men on a yellow shore. All in black swim trunks. Their faces were almost the way a kid would draw them—a line for a nose, a straight line for a mouth, and the eyes were two round orbs, unformed hollows seeming to look inward to loss and grief and outward to infinity. The three men looked stunned, as though realizing something that was never realized before. While all around, the water was exploding in black, yellow, green, brown.

"I lowered myself onto a bench. David Park, Helen's father. We had finally come face-to-face.

"My eyes moved to the upper right. His signature up there in small letters. Not cursive, a printed capital *P,* small *a-r-k.* And then the number '58.

"Sitting in front of *Four Men*—then standing, putting my nose close to the paint, then standing back, again sitting down on the bench, leaning forward, elbows on knees, head in hands." I did these motions in class. "All other paintings faded. I was pulled into one large existence. Time was spread out in the painting. Here was summer in eternity.

"I called Helen across the country from a corner pay phone right after I left the museum.

"'Oh, Natalie,' and I could see her, seeing that painting in her mind. 'It was David's first one-man show in New York City. The inaugural opening of the Staempfli Gallery. We all flew out—me; my sister, Natalie; David and Lydia.'

"'The Whitney purchased it at that show. It was the most money David ever got for a painting. We were all so excited. We went out to dinner to celebrate.'

"I had to ask. 'Helen, how much did it sell for?'

"'Oh, Natalie, they were such innocent times. It was sold for a thousand dollars.'"

I paused a long moment, standing in front of the class. "David died two years later." The students held their breath. "So it's time to view the man who was David Park's best friend."

The class flew apart.

Through words and story I seduced them over to no words— to color, form, and space. They were hungry now to discover face-to-face the abstract art of Richard Diebenkorn, better known by close friends as Dick.

13

The Lineage of Literature

Sitting in the third row, fourth seat in Mr. Cates's tenth-grade English class, I held *The Ballad of the Sad Café,* the seventy-page novella by Carson McCullers, in my young hands.

It was an October day in Farmingdale, Long Island, but the peach trees were blossoming in Georgia in the wide and painful terrain of this book. From the very first paragraph—how can I say this?—every dark word on every white page penetrated my mind, clearing it of superfluous thoughts. My early life disappeared into the language of "Miss McCullers," as Mr. Cates called her, and my aching heart found a larger aching, a bigger, more hollow, echoing receptacle. I was Miss Amelia; I was Cousin Lymon; I even became cruel and dejected Marvin Macy. I empathized with each character. I have never forgotten them or their names.

Miss Amelia, who never married, except for ten disastrous days to Marvin Macy, lived alone above the café and general store where she sold her famous homemade brew and some staples, such as meal, snuff, and animal feed. Six feet two inches tall, with muscles like a man's and eyes slightly crossed, she was a shrewd businesswoman, had a passion for lawsuits, and enjoyed curing people of whatever ailed them. She developed her own remedies and administered care in her back office for no fee at all.

At almost midnight on an April evening, with five locals sitting on Miss Amelia's porch and the street deserted, a lonely little hunchback appeared down the road. He was childlike, ugly, and destitute. For no apparent reason Miss Amelia moved him upstairs to her three rooms, where no one else had ever been.

That meeting of the two of them began the tale. The entry of Marvin Macy, gone for many years, just out of the state penitentiary for robbery and suspicion of murder, completed the strange triumvirate.

When Miss Amelia and Marvin Macy finally greased up to fight each other, first exchanging blows and, after half an hour of punches, locked into a wrestling hold, the terrible test of strength neared a climax.

Reading about her hoarse breaths, her strong hands at his throat, I felt frightened and jolted. I had never encountered anything like this before: the sheer physicality of the two, a man and a woman, faced off in something having nothing to do with love, except as an energy twisted to a force of dead rage and power.

This was a lot to take in for a young suburban girl. I reeled from the fight. My eyes squeezed shut; I gritted my teeth and something screamed in my head. *Yes, yes.*

I've since been told, Don't get stuck on the finger pointing to the moon when you want the moon. But even then, after reading *The Ballad of the Sad Café,* I didn't want the moon. It was enough to have the finger that knew to point. I needed words in and of themselves, those glittering beings that woke this neglected kid from her sleepy haze so long ago. Someone, finally, was talking to me.

Every day I saw the sadness of my mother, the weariness of my hardworking grandparents, the meanness of my World War II–veteran father, and the desolation of the men he served shots to in his bar. This was not a pretty world, but it was a different part of the world rendered real by Miss McCullers. She had written *The Ballad of the Sad Café* when she was twenty-five years old. How could someone of that age know these things? But it's not always age that teaches us; sometimes the wounded heart of a person who knows how to write is enough.

She also showed me this: to love is a frightening thing. We are pulled two ways: to stay closed and protect ourselves versus our boundless need to meet our nature. If we look at the state of the world, shutting down seems logical. But to truly live we have no choice but to keep unfolding, even in the face of devastation.

After my mother died, my sister couldn't bear selling her old house in Greenacres, near Lake Worth, so for two years we negotiated. That word sounds far too sane. Eventually I put a lien on the house. My mother's lawyer refused to ever again do business with my sister. She was feral, distrustful, sure someone was cheating her—that I had no right to the small inheritance we were to share. Eventually she got a mortgage and bought the house.

She wanted everything intact. A mausoleum. I shipped home two of my grandmother's chairs and one small side cabinet and left everything else for her.

Each year for the past three years I've gone down to Florida to pay homage to constant summer, humidity, palm trees, and alligators. I eat a single meal at the deli near my parents' house and then drift down Lake Avenue to Hoffman's Chocolates.

This year, though, I take things more slowly. My girlfriend, Baksim, and I drive through the neighborhood, marveling at the houses lined in a row, all exactly alike. I park at the swimming pool and we walk the three blocks down to Ambertree Lane. Then we sit on the small brick wall in front of the door to the house and note how the wandering Jew plants grow unchecked across the walkway. I feel content to sit here for several minutes. Finally I step up to the brown door and ring the bell, put my ear to the metal surface, and hear it ring in the empty house. I ring it again and again. "Mommy," I call out. "Mommy. It's me. Open the door."

I want to go in badly. I haven't been in there for four years, and my sister, though she punctually pays the monthly mortgage, has not been there either. The neighbor across the street checks on it periodically. From what I've heard from the occasional terse e-mails I receive from my sister, the roof is leaking and the ceiling needs work. She hoped to rent it out year-round, but so far only a single man comes down for three months each winter. She has never met him. He is supposed to be very clean and has rearranged my mother's furniture. I want in, but I've left the key in the top drawer in my kitchen back in New Mexico. I've done this deliberately, to protect myself from these moments. I no longer own this house. Technically it would be breaking in.

"Why don't you go across the street to the neighbor?" Baksim suggests. "Maybe she'll let you in."

I hesitate.

"Go over and just say hello."

There's a Christmas wreath on the door, and a lawn full of glittering deer, and a sled and a fat Santa Claus. I ring the bell, and the door opens.

At first Daisy doesn't recognize me. I mention my mother's name. "Oh, yes." She is friendly. "Would you like to go in? You're family. Meet me at the side door. I'll get the key."

That was easy, I think, and we walk back across the street. She hands me the key and, voilà, I step in.

Every piece of furniture has been moved flat against some wall. No sitting arrangements, no conviviality. There's a water stain on my mother's dining room table and a batch of black ants on the white tile floor by the two windows. The ceiling paper is curling; water has dripped through, right at the threshold to her bedroom. All shutters are closed, and the air conditioning is on low to avoid mildew but not enough to cool.

I get out quickly. No life in there.

When Baksim and I get back to the hotel, I am paralyzed, remembering the evening walks to the pool alone after my father died, my mother ensconced in her chair in front of the TV she played loudly but could no longer hear or see clearly. The rough cement sidewalk on my bare feet, towel over my shoulder, sun setting too early in late November. I climb over the wall—the pool gate is locked at dusk—and look around. Then I peel off my bathing suit and dive into the dark water, confident that none of the seniors, who rarely show even in the daytime, will dare come now.

Then the dreaded walk back to the little box house on the corner. I replay that walk: entering the dark house, the gray light from the screen cast on my mother's face. She does not stir, and I lie down in the guest bedroom on the carpeted floor, where I've made a little bed of my grandmother's quilt—the frame of the sofa that opens to a bed has collapsed long ago. But first I close the door, turn off the air conditioning, open the metal shades and windows, positing that I am the only one in the five-hundred-unit community who performs this daring act, letting the cool, heavy air waft in.

. . .

Baksim grew up poor in Hong Kong, where she didn't go to school until she was ten, and only then because her mother had managed to marry a British soldier stationed there in the fifties, after the war. Her stepfather sent her to a British school in Hong Kong, where she didn't speak a lick of English and she had her first pair of shoes and the other schoolmates made fun of her because she was Chinese. When she complained at home to her mother, the advice was "fight back."

She waited until each one of the three bullies was alone to take her revenge. With those shoes—her mother made them for her too large, intending them to last, with strong metal around the rim—she kicked each of her taunters hard in the butt. The last one, the leader, was a heavy British girl with thick glasses. The girl fell to the floor crying. Baksim was about to smash her glasses with her shoes but instead said, "I'm sorry I hurt you," realizing her enemy was in pain. After that they became fast friends, the little Asian girl and the fleshy white Brit who towered over her.

When her mother first met her stepfather, Baksim was farmed out to a poor family at age seven for two years. Her mother was afraid the English soldier wouldn't want her if she had a child.

Baksim's adopted family ate one bowl of rice a day and some salted fish. When they sat at the table, they kept their feet raised on the chair rungs. Rats came out at dinner and wandered under the table, hoping a crumb or morsel would be dropped. Barefoot, thin as a wire, she wandered the streets. The ghetto people called her "the wooden beauty" because she was so sad.

After her mother couldn't get pregnant in England, she confessed to her new husband that she had a little girl left in Hong Kong. Her husband flew back and appeared at the door of the boarding house. Baksim was standing in the hall when the owner opened the door to this tall white westerner. He told her to call him Daddy and yelled at the man that her mother sent monthly checks for her care, yet she was filthy and starving.

The next day he took her to the movies to see *One Hundred and One Dalmatians*. She sat next to him with one fist full of popcorn and the other gripping chocolate malted milk balls.

Now, after thirty years on Wall Street, Baksim treats me to the Breakers, this hotel on the beach, first built in 1896 by oil, real estate, and railroad tycoon Henry Flagler to accommodate travelers on his Florida East Coast Railway. It burned down twice, and in 1925 the contractors abandoned the wooden construction for fireproof concrete. They built a 550-room replacement after the Villa Medici in Rome, complete with a large lobby ceiling painted by a classically trained New York City artist. The building and grounds occupy 140 acres along the Atlantic Ocean.

Out the large window in our room on the fifth floor we can see the panoramic curve of the beach as the waves roll in. Wave upon wave, breaking onshore. At night when we open the windows we smell the salt air and feel in the black expanse all the distant places you can travel to, all the multitudinous stars sparkling over it all. McCullers wrote, "A weaver might look up suddenly and see for the first time the cold, weird radiance of a midnight January sky, and a deep fright at his own smallness stop his heart."

McCullers showed me bone-chilling betrayal and crushing abandonment. Like much great literature, it pointed to something right in front of our noses: there is no cure for human life, except to live it, being willing to rip off blinders as we go and let the light in.

Losing

It is only me now
and I do not fit in my own shoes

The mountain is mine
Moonlight and the faraway call
of the train—all mine

But who stares at me in the window?

My dead father has hollow eyes;
and grief—that old lover—
is mine too

14

In the Crossing

(for Ann Filemyr)

My father's just home from work, his long white sleeves rolled up, a thin belt at his waist, pleated gray pants. He leans back in our backyard, bends his right arm at an angle and flings the rubber ball as high as his powerful arm will let him.

We both lean our heads back, calculating where it will come down. Take two steps this way, two steps the other way. Hands cupped in front of us, measuring the speed, the exact spot—*wham* into both my hands.

I throw it to him, and again he leans back and flings that ball into the early June evening air. The crickets not yet sounding, the steak barbecuing next-door at the Carosellas'. "Vinnie Carosella doesn't play ball with his daughter," my mother yells from the kitchen window. "Buddy, Natalie is going to hurt her womanly insides."

I want to play through the night, and even my father is fascinated. How far could he really toss this thing? In one shot the ball seems to disappear into the clouds.

He climbs up on the outdoor redwood furniture, first the

bench and then the table—the umbrella hasn't been put in the center hole yet—and he tosses it ever higher.

My mother hisses through the screen, "The neighbors are going to think we're crazy." He tosses it again. My sister, with her brown curls, three years younger, is somewhere in the background and is the only one listening to my mother.

Now that he throws it from the table I have to lean over to find its landing point. I run into a corner of the house and a tooth begins to bleed. The blood is running down my arm. My blue T-shirt has red blotches. It doesn't hurt, so I ignore it. The amazing thing: my father doesn't notice.

Richard, the younger Carosella boy, yells, "Nice throw," and my father turns his head and preens.

I want that ball in my two hands more than God, more than Double Bubble, more than a licorice stick or the new blue three-speed bike I'll get this summer.

You want to know what happened to the tooth, the blood? You want to know who noticed? What *I* want to know is how come I can't have it all back. The sweet corn bleeding with yellow butter and salt, the beefsteak tomatoes, the Sealtest cherry vanilla ice cream, the bing cherries. Shooting watermelon's black pits across the table, a contest for how many ears of corn eaten. You try to beat my father—once he ate eighteen to win against Uncle Sam, his skinny brother. If my uncle hadn't stopped at seventeen, my father would have eaten more. He would not lose. His veins were shot through with the slow coursing motor of a boat in idle, waiting to shift into gear.

Wham. Into my hands again. The highest shot returned to me. I scream; I am victorious. My father glances down. "Oh, my God. Natalie, what happened?" I grin ear to ear.

He grabs my arm, drags me to the screen door. "Sylvia, get a towel." She glances out the window and runs down the stairs.

My grandparents are behind her. My grandmother's right cheek is clasped in her right hand. "Have you gone crazy?"

My eyes dart from one to another. "I caught the ball."

They look at one another over my head. "What should we do?"

"The emergency room," my father says. He runs for car keys.

Now I am trembling and quiet.

A two-hour calamity, four stitches, and it is over. I still have all of my teeth.

But the bigger problem is not solved. Where did my father go?

Walk with me down Main Street in fall. Stuffed ghosts and scarecrows leaning against the hardware store windows. Walk farther, past the stationer's. Von Leessen's across the street—homemade ice cream. Walk farther to the library on the corner. Across Conklin is the brick Aero Tavern, wrought iron framing the many squares of windows. Inside, behind the bar backed by the light of a Seagram's twirling mirror and rows of liquor bottles and a stand of bagged pretzels and Wise potato chips, is the person I'm looking for. Always in an oxford shirt with the sleeves rolled up to midforearm. It's Ben Goldberg. He is still young here.

A few dry leaves drop to the ground off the elms and crackle in the gutter when stepped on. My father walks out the front door with the green bag in his hand. He's going across to the other corner, where the bank is, to deposit last night's earnings. He stops in the cigar store, picks up *Newsday* and the *Daily News*, buys four Bering Plaza cigars. Then pauses. Marshmallow witches and sugar corn for Halloween are displayed on the counter. *The girls would like those.* We, my sister and I, are *the girls,* and he is thinking about us. It's not often, but how sweet when he does. He buys some trick-or-treat candy and then crosses the street. When he's in the crossing, right in the middle, I want to yell, "*Stop! Don't you know you'll die and someday leave us?*" But it never enters his mind. He's young, maybe forty. Death is another country. His father died at sixty-eight; his mother of Parkinson's at sixty-five. But they are buried in a Jewish cemetery, a forty-minute drive down the Southern State Parkway.

This is months before February, when he buys us cakes and cupcakes for Valentine's Day, and we, all three of us—Rhoda, me, and his wife, Sylvia—are his Valentines.

After he died—seven months after—I was driving a moving van up the interstate in the snow to St. Paul, Minnesota, and stopped for gas and remembered it was February 14. No more cakes from Daddy. He did it only twice in my childhood, but the occasions stuck. I cried the rest of the way into the outskirts of the Twin Cities.

15

Losing Katherine

After two days in Paris, still jet-lagged, we rent a car to drive down to the retreat center where I will teach. The estimated travel time is two and a half hours. But at the Orléans exit an hour south of Paris, I veer off the highway. I want to see the town whose name is referred to repeatedly in Paris: Porte d'Orléans, a subway stop; Velodrome d'Orléans, for cycling races; below the clock at Musée d'Orsay, Paris-Orléans; a dock called Quai d'Orléans.

My assistant—a longtime student, wife of a rabbi, and PhD in art history—and I will have some *fun*. I keep repeating that word, strange to a Jew, but I consider it important. This is it. This one great life. Let's take some pleasure, even when this Orléans turns out not to be much of anything: bland streets, one cathedral, one nasty tea shop—the only one open at 3:00 P.M. But we make the most of it: we go to their one *musée des beaux-arts*, which has a Gauguin and a slab of a hind leg of raw animal meat painted by Soutine and a quiet Corot we forget as soon as we pass it. But still, name a town in North Dakota that has anything equal. And there are fresh peaches in the market here in June, not to be seen till August in New Mexico.

The problem is we can't manage to drive out of the town. Around and around we go, with no map. Forget the GPS on Saundra's iPhone. *You are here,* a metallic female voice repeats when we face a dead-end street at the edge of a river bluff. *You have arrived.* Very Zen of her but not helpful.

But at last I am relieved of the burden of planning—this retreat has been in the works for almost two years. Justine, another longtime student, has a French grandmother who has a retreat center that her uncle, a conductor in Paris, developed for musicians. They've taken a barn and made it acoustically perfect for concerts. We will use it as a zendo. The first Sit, Walk, Write: True Secret Retreat ever on European soil. Many American students— and also ones from Canada and the Netherlands—signed up within a week. One student gave a donation for several fellowships. The stipulation: they must be longtime students who could never imagine—or afford—coming across the ocean. I called four in the winter evenings and told them to pack their bags.

Justine's father was a serious Zen practitioner under the famous Zen teacher Taisen Deshimaru. He was delighted this was happening on his mother's farm.

Saundra and I manage to arrive at Villefavard twelve hours late, just before the nearby Protestant church clangs out twelve midnight gongs. Then Saundra confesses she has been nervous the whole time, a natural Jewish state of mind. The lights are out and we tramp up the steps. Soon we drop into a sleep disconnected from country or the twirling Earth.

Two nights later, about to begin the retreat, I am met at the bottom of the steps by Steve, a burly, tall, ponytailed man who has studied with me before. The twilight is casting a yellow glow on his face and on everything around us. He tells me, "Aunt Katie has hit her head, and she lay unconscious for eight hours before they found her. She's in the hospital. The blood thinned by the pills she took for her heart condition seeped into her brain."

I grab the front of his shirt and lean into his chest. He is the nephew of my dear friend Katherine Thanas, who is eighty-five, insistently independent, living alone in her own apartment. Bloody Kleenex was found upstairs—they figure she tried to minister to herself. Whenever it was that she went downstairs, she blacked out.

A black chasm opens in front of me: we are losing her. Through muffled sobs, I manage, "Any chance?"

"None." Her nephew chokes on that single word.

I'd seen her last in early January. I had brought her bright red-blue-black striped wool socks.

"Katherine, we need to jazz you up." She wore white cotton toe-fitted ones for the zendo's highly shined wood floor. Traditional Japanese.

She laughed. "These won't fit. I'm size eleven."

"You've got to be kidding. We'll go to the men's store."

"We can try. They won't be as colorful."

We found her shocking-pink-and-black-striped socks at a corner shoe store.

"Warm," she said, delighted. It was freezing cold in her apartment. The usual California attitude: a denial that it ever gets cold, so the housing is miserably insulated and heated.

We ate at a Japanese restaurant. She'd been on an absolute no-fat—not even olive oil—diet for three years. The doctor said it would help her heart. He also said no one could follow such a stringent protocol. That, along with weekly energy work, turned her heart around. No open-heart surgery. The doctor was amazed.

· · ·

I met Katherine in the late eighties, around the time my Zen teacher was dying. She visited him in Minneapolis. He was one of her teachers when he first came to America to help Suzuki Roshi in the early years of San Francisco Zen Center.

"He was not a good example. He was too perfect." She lifted her elbows to show how erect his *gassho* was.

Or maybe I met her first after he died and she asked me to do a benefit for her small community. The money they made from the writing workshop would build a bathroom for the zendo, formerly a Chinese laundry.

She picked me up in her manual-drive Honda at Yvonne Rand's home in Muir Beach, and we crossed the Golden Gate Bridge, continuing southwest, down to her shoulder of the peninsula. As we drove the long highways, her energetic foot pounced on the clutch.

Five years later was my true meeting with her. I had taught writing for a week at Tassajara Zen Monastery and was given a week on my own, in exchange, to soak in the springs and stay in a new stone guesthouse. I was teaching myself to do abstract paintings. Form detached from meaning, meaning expressed in color. I had six cheap oil pastels and an even cheaper packet of 8 x 11 sheets of paper.

Katherine was there that week at Tassajara, leading a Zen and yoga retreat. She had lived at Tassajara for many winters after the summer guests left. That's when Zen students faced the wall for long hours, far away from city distractions, settling deep into remote silence.

She leaned over my shoulder as I sat on the dirt path looking up at the waterfall. "Not quite abstract—not realistic, either." She pointed her index finger along the blue line.

"What was it like to study with Diebenkorn?"

"I knew I couldn't be great. I was pulled to Zen."

That week I sought her out. I practiced Zen with all of my heart but loved writing and painting. At that time they were still opposing each other. Katherine knew about both.

She came up behind me on the third day, her fingers pointing up at the tree, my finger smeared with brown. "I like this line. But you don't have it yet."

"Why don't you paint anymore?" I asked her.

She laughed and said nothing.

I can hear her voice. Whenever she picked up the phone there was delight in it, ready to take on any person on the other end. No small talk—how was your relationship, your job, your feelings about your cousin? She wanted the truthful deep answers below polite chatter. She joined you in any challenge, always wanting to understand what it is to be human. Right until the end, at that January sushi lunch. "I don't understand relationships," I said. She gave me a jaunty sigh and a head shake. Nothing ironic. And then she asked the most surprising thing: "How do you know love?"

Even that last visit, I could not keep up with her darting up the stairs. And she insisted on driving. She had another version of her old manual Honda, and we careened around the many corners of her tight neighborhood.

We call back to the States the first night, the second night. Each day, Katherine is still in the hospital.

A year earlier she had visited me in Santa Fe and popped up after each meal to clear her plate. "Don't wash the dishes. You'll make more of a mess. Katherine, you can relax and let me do the work."

"I want to be useful." Always the Zen practitioner: when you can no longer work, you can no longer eat. We were brought up on the raw edge of Japanese ancient teachings, transmitted through great human effort, challenging all adversity.

On that visit she brought a gift of not only Kenzaburo Oe's *A Personal Matter* but also a memoir by Oe's English translator John Nathan, whom she knew. "I wish John had written less about his life and more about what it's like to translate." She tapped the cover. "But interesting just the same."

It was typical of her. A fresh slant on the novel—the translator. She read widely, and it showed in the curious bent of her mind. No matter how nonchalant or vague you might be in a particular moment, she came back at you.

That visit in New Mexico, her nose bled from the altitude. It was the blood thinners. The same ones that came to get her, even though she did not eat a drop of fat.

We gather wildflowers in the French countryside to make a fat bouquet, plant it in the middle of the retreat circle with her name on a placard.

Steve tells us, "Aunt Katie sent me Rilke, Charles Olson, Laurens van der Post, three of Natalie's books, Jack Kornfield, Norm Fischer. My whole childhood she sent me books. I'm a writer today because of that.

"She had a great sense of humor. Just three years ago I wanted to see her zendo. She showed me around—then, in front of the altar, she jumped up, kicking her heels together. 'I'm the abbot, I'm the abbot,' she sang out.

"But she could also be tough. I wore a weird long, multi-colored coat and she told me straightaway it looked terrible, that I didn't need to freak people out."

I smile. Katherine had told me that conversation in detail and had worried she hadn't handled it well.

Back in January we had talked about her coming to this French retreat. "You could relax, look at cows, eat baguettes—no cheese—and once during the week you could give a single dharma talk to my students."

Three days into the retreat they take her off life support. Miraculously, she keeps breathing. Her students convince the hospital to let her go home and be on hospice, surrounded twenty-four hours a day by people who love her.

Each night after the last class session, Steve and I stand in the stone courtyard, near tall grass pastures, clumps of brown Limousin cows in the distance, and try to call California in their early morning, almost half a globe away. Often our cell phone can't make contact. We stand in the darkening shade, hearing electric noise, clasping the metal to our ears.

Katherine was the only one in the dharma world who, after reading *The Great Failure*—my memoir about finding out after he died that my Zen teacher had been sleeping with students—called me and directly said she didn't like it. No one else spoke to me; they all silently disappeared. But after our call, Katherine and I did not see each other for four years. I was sorely aware of that rift and calculated from a distance her aging.

Then one day the phone rang: "Younger students have been reading your book and telling me, 'It's really good.' I thought: *Am I not a Zen teacher? I must be open-minded.* I reread it. I got it all wrong the first time. I was blinded. When can we see each other?"

I was in Santa Cruz on a book tour soon after. We ate Japanese for dinner, as we always did, and she sat in the front row at the reading. I was grateful to be reconnected.

Once I asked her to conduct a three-day meditation retreat in the solar adobe zendo I'd just built in Taos.

Each day she gave a lecture. "I rented a car at the airport in Albuquerque. Getting to Taos was fine—only one highway pointing north—but then I had to follow Natalie's directions on these dirt back roads. I got lost. I realize now that when I listened to her over the phone, I pictured in my mind what she was saying, and when the markers appeared in actuality—for instance, the right at an abandoned adobe—they weren't how I'd pictured them, so I ignored them and went looking for what matched my vision. Isn't that how we also work in our life? We don't see reality."

The last evening in France, just before the students break silence, Steve comes up to me and whispers in my ear, "I just spoke to my brother. Katherine let go."

I nod and proceed to the zendo in a trance.

I'm unable to recall anything I taught that night. But these forty students traveled far to be with me. I have to fulfill my obligation—garner my energy—even though someone I love has slowly been dying far away.

So many times this has happened. I am teaching while something important is happening somewhere else.

That night, after the ending ceremony and festivities, in the long early hours past midnight, alone in the third story of a French farmhouse, I fall into the unformed chasm of grief.

The next morning, still in my clothes, I hear a hesitant knock at my door. "It's past breakfast and class is in five minutes." Saundra, whom I twirled on that twelve-hour drive down, opens the door a crack.

"I can't do it," I growl. "You teach."

A flicker of hesitation. Then she sees my face. "I couldn't be with her," I cry.

. . .

When I leave the retreat, I walk for seven days in the Dordogne Valley, through fields of corn; among walnut trees, sunflowers; and at the edge of a wide, swollen, meandering river. So much in bloom.

We are no different from a flower, I think. It gives off its radiance—then dies. We don't expect that same flower to come back next June. Another takes its place.

But there must also be something else. My rambunctious friend, where are you now? Wherever you are, there is still so much to say.

> Bright pink zinnia
> my friend Katherine
> one candle burning

16

BJ

Filmmaker Mary Feidt and I went up to Hibbing, Minnesota, on the Iron Range, a four-hour drive north of the Twin Cities, to see if we could discover Bob Dylan's roots, to explore where he came from and how it influenced who he was now.

We went in December. The filmmaker wanted to see the place at its peak darkness, to see the juxtaposition of Bob's Jewish religion and Christmas lights. Film is visual, and we needed pictures. Besides, when you go that far north in Minnesota, life is about weather—the extreme cold and how you survive, how you make peace with it, how you make it yours. We met Bob Dylan's childhood best friend and the drummer in his first band, when Bob was sixteen. We found the home he lived in, saw the synagogue where fifty Jewish families worshipped together in the fifties. We met classmates who still lived in Hibbing, and found the cousin of his high school girlfriend, Echo Helstrom.

When we met BJ Rolfzen, Bob Dylan's high school English teacher, Mary told me she knew we had a film. Bright blue eyes, eighty-one years old, sitting next to a decorated tree in his living room, he opened an old well-worn anthology and read us the poem by William Carlos Williams "This Is Just to Say." The poet leaves a note to his wife: forgive me for eating the plums; they were so cold and so delicious.

Then BJ gave us a lesson: "This poem doesn't make a lot of sense unless you look at the title." Then he went on his own riff of a poem: "This is just to say, Bill, I'm glad you are my son / This is just to say, Leona, I'm glad you married me fifty-four years ago. . . ." We tasted what it must have been like to be in his classroom as he leaned over, his eyes burning into ours: "Thomas Carlyle called poetry 'an open secret.' Do you know what that means?"

This English teacher loved poetry from the inside out, with his blood and muscle, not as some intellectual exercise. Robert Zimmerman, later known as Dylan, hadn't been alone up there. He had been fed by this extraordinary human being.

"Thirty-five years in the classroom. That was my life," he said.

"Did you miss teaching when you retired?" I asked.

"Oh, no. I have a motor scooter, and in the spring and summer, I pack a lunch and ride out to the woods with my books. I lie under the trees and read poems."

Three hours later we reluctantly left him. When we looked back, we saw a small, light-gray clapboard house, deep in snow across from the Assumption Catholic School; but we felt like we'd been in some grand canyon with verse echoing off the walls.

We returned to Hibbing again in June, wanting to see what it was like in summer. Mary wanted to shoot me riding behind BJ on his motor scooter. He'd had a stroke a few years back. His hand and foot were affected, but he had figured out a way to still ride his bike, adding a third wheel for steadiness.

He drove me through the old Hibbing. The town had been moved in the thirties. Rich iron ore was discovered under the town site, so the mining company paid the residents to relocate. Old street signs, curbs, and the crumbling library could still be seen in overgrown green grass. We rode out to the taconite mines, the whole time shouting poetry to each other and laughing.

BJ took me to his old classroom in Hibbing High School: room 204. He showed me the front row, third seat, where Robert Zimmerman sat. "He was a quiet boy. Very courteous. He got a good look at me from this seat." He tapped the desktop. "And I got a good look at him."

"Did you know then who he would become?" I asked.

"At that age it's too young to tell."

Back at his house, in his basement office, he played Dylan's music for me, loud. "'Gotta Serve Somebody.' I love that song," he said. He jacked the sound up some more with the remote. "It was created to be played this way," he yelled over the singing.

Later we sat in his dining room over coffee, which his wife, Leona, served weak, with walnut bread and cookies on a white tablecloth, silver laid out beside them. Again BJ played Dylan songs, this time from *Time Out of Mind*. The music blasted over the fine dining setting.

He quoted from a song of his old student: "'I was born here and I'll die here against my will.' Me too." He thumped his chest with his left hand. "I like it here. They can keep the other side. This side is for me."

Then he recited a poem he'd written after his stroke:

Two Crows

The road which once I traveled by
Listening to the song of the meadowlark
Now echoes with the cry of the crow.

He finished reciting and stared at me.

"That's penetrating," was all I could say.

He gave me his self-published memoir, *The Spring of My Life*, which I read when I returned home. He'd been brought up in the center of Minnesota in a small town during the Depression. He slept across the feet of his three older brothers on a mattress made of straw that stunk of urine. A snowdrift often formed over him, blown in through a hole in the wall. Too cold to sleep, he'd get up and wander downstairs, but it wasn't any warmer there. He did terribly in school. He was always hungry and never did his homework because there was no place at home to do it. Even at meals some of them had to stand—there weren't enough chairs.

"Did you read a lot?" I asked BJ when I saw him next, a few months later.

"Never. I was trying to survive."

He began to read when he joined the military. He never drank. His father was a drunk who couldn't keep a job. Once his father tried to commit suicide. He didn't succeed, but he was disabled permanently and couldn't support his family.

When BJ was a kid, he lost half of his shoe in a snowbank, and he wired the two parts back together in the school basement. Referring to that experience, he wrote this beautiful poem in adulthood:

> *Autobiography*
>
> Walking
> in the snow
> wearing half a
> shoe
> searching for
> William Shakespeare

He said he could have made a career in the military, but he wanted to go back to school. He wanted to become a teacher. "A teacher was a star illuminating a dark night." In all of his years of teaching, he never took a sabbatical, because he couldn't leave his students. He told me that he had never had a good teacher himself, not even at the university.

His social studies teacher in college began each class by pulling down a map at the front of the room but never used it. As an eager young student in his twenties, BJ was waiting to be shown something there. "Then he'd put his notes down on the podium and lecture. If he got too far in front of the stand, he couldn't say anything. He only relied on notes. It was disgusting."

We traveled back to Hibbing several more times and made the film *Tangled Up in Bob*. At the end I realized I couldn't find Bob Dylan, the man I played on my stereo, in Hibbing. What I found in Hibbing was Bobby Zimmerman, who eventually gave birth to Bob Dylan. Hibbing was where he came from, but he left and went on to another life.

For Dylan's sixty-fifth birthday on May 24, 2006, Mary and I traveled up to Hibbing again to show the film. BJ was nervous. I'd written to him that he had a large part. He wrote me several times, saying he was going to leave town. Mostly I thought he was joking about his discomfort.

When we arrived in Hibbing, I found out that the whole last month he'd had trouble sleeping. He feared what his colleagues would think, this man with a wild heart and mind, an awake human being. He'd managed to survive in small-town America by working hard, attending church, caring earnestly for his four children, and trying not to stand out, not to draw attention, except by being a memorable teacher. And now we had arrived from another country, New Mexico, and were recognizing him, pointing him out, making him the star of our film.

The first time he saw himself on the large screen, he was apprehensive, curious, astonished.

We showed it again two days later. This time he was more relaxed and congratulated Mary on her professionalism. He told me the next day that people seemed to like it. He was relieved.

When I said good-bye to BJ at the end of the week, he was not naive. We had been traveling a long way to a small town for a purpose.

"I'm going to miss you," he told me. "And the sound of your name will always bring back special memories."

I wanted to shift the uncomfortable moment and quickly say I'd be back. But I didn't say it. I told him I loved him. He was now eighty-three. The year before he had fallen and fought for weeks to come back from the brink. The measure of time changes for a man like this.

The film turned out gorgeous, and something large and unexpected happened to me in the process. I went up to Hibbing hoping to find home—Dylan's, mine, somebody's. But you can't find a home in a house, a building, a place. Instead I found friendship, with the breath of poetry breathing us, both BJ and me.

17

Old Zendo

I'm back in the old zendo, the one on Cerro Gordo Road in Santa Fe, adjacent to the stupa. A square room, white-plastered adobe walls, wood floor, a skylight overhead in the center. I'm sitting in the corner on a Thursday night. The sitting has already started with six people. But this is not the old Zen, not strict. I can find my place even though I've come in late.

In 1984 Baker Roshi taught here. Philip Whalen, the great poet/priest, would sit opposite me; Issan, who eventually became the abbot for the San Francisco Hartford Street Zen Center, with his head shaved, was to my right; a stodgy, delightful woman named Miriam Bobkoff sat diagonal to me in black robes. An ex–prize fighter, muscles bulging, sat a few cushions away, and also a young man with a long beard named Robert Sycamore. Baker had recently resigned from San Francisco Zen Center for indiscretions that at the time were unclear, and this was the part of his group that had followed him.

In 1984 I had just returned to New Mexico from practicing at the Minnesota Zen Center. Wherever Zen was, near where I lived, I went.

Besides, I liked Baker. I was not part of the brouhaha and felt comfortable continuing to like him. I was in that heaven place before my own perfect teacher's betrayals were discovered. At that point I ignored—or tried to ignore—anything that got in my way, not knowing then that the obstacles were part of the way and I needed to figure out what—or what not—to do with them.

Now it's twenty-four years later, mid-March. The wind is moaning outside. The wind will go on well into May. Spring is a miserable season in New Mexico. But you should have seen the twilight as my ten-year-old Volvo bumped along the dirt road. Soft, gray-blue, and big. Tentative, lonesome, home.

The day before, our small group had messed around with a koan about mending. Two Zen friends from old China have a discussion, and you almost think one of them gets it right, but then you realize it's not quite like that. You can't hold one side and forget the other.

I left the Quaker Meeting House on Canyon Road, where we have these koan salons every Wednesday afternoon from three to five. It has nothing to do with the Quakers—they lend us this beautiful but cold room. And we sit huddled even though the heater—too far away—is blasting.

Joan Sutherland, who leads these salons, hardly says a word, but this time out of frustration I turn to her. "Speak or we won't come back."

She laughs but gives us a heavy hint.

I'm suddenly desolate. It makes the koan worse, even if I understand better. My whole body wants to be involved. It is like pointing out a person across the room and saying, "Someday you'll love him." No help at all. I have to find my own way to him and into love.

The rest of the group was delighted by the help.

I was miserable. That's how I ended up the next night in the zendo. I don't usually go on Thursday nights. I was hungry and at the same time felt trapped.

Not only had my mother died in December but the man next door to me died the next day, and my landlord in the house behind took his last tough breath a few weeks later, and a forty-eight-year-old I cared about in New York surprised me and died too. All at once no one was sick and got better. They stopped breathing for good.

You would have liked Sandy, the ninety-four-year-old retired surgeon I paid rent to. He'd pass my kitchen door in the passenger's seat—Louise, his wife of forty years, drove their station wagon—and I'd come out and lean into his window, and the three of us would chat.

"Do you see that bird's nest on top of that telephone pole?" He pointed.

I'd have to squint hard. "Yes, you're right. Wow."

He was clear almost to the end. I'd stop by, bring watermelon— his favorite—out of season, while he was propped up in bed reading the *New York Times*.

Gone now. A rush of death in a month's time.

It was the forty-eight-year-old in New York who was the hardest for me. I'd walk down Camino del Monte Sol at the edge of the road and whisper, "Adele, I am so sorry," and there was no consolation. My stomach in a tight fist against that other place that I feared was no place, only a hole a body is dropped into. No more Natalie. Or Mr. Digneo next door.

I remember going to Baker during retreat. "I get sick of my thoughts, but every time I become present, the fear is so great it drives me into panicked thoughts again. I'm afraid of being nothing."

"That's the main dilemma for most of us."

Another time, after I learned my teacher in Minneapolis was going to die, I went to Baker. He had experienced the death of a teacher when Suzuki Roshi died and passed the lineage on to him. "How did you handle Suzuki's death? I'm going to so miss Katagiri."

"Oh, I didn't miss him. I had to step up and do his job."

"You didn't miss him?"

He shook his head.

I left that day thinking, *That's not me*. My heart was so broken, but I miss that time. It was good to love someone that much.

Now I'm caught in the dark web of a koan, a conversation, an interchange from more than a thousand years ago.

I'm missing the point of the interchange because my mind is too complicated. There's no trick. It's right in front of me. I can't see it. You say water and I hear mud. You say dead and I say wake them up. I say I am sixty years old and I don't accept it. Then I have a huge sense of urgency. I have to fill in every inch of the next ten years. And the anxiety intensifies. Where will all of this lead? I suspect the truth is not one way or the other. It is both: I am alive and I will die.

18

Lost Purse

"I have something you want," a woman called out in the last moment of a weekend writing workshop in Lenox, Massachusetts.

Jerking my head to the left, I found the body to the voice—in her fifties, short-cropped salt-and-pepper hair, slightly built.

"You found my purse?" I squealed into the microphone. The purse was small, gold, knit by a friend. I use it to hold my room key and loose change at these gatherings.

I had lost it the day before when I went swimming, plopped it someplace and forgot it. Peeled off my shorts and dove into the wide August lake surrounded by tall trees with my friend and coteacher Sean Murphy. We had to swim far into the interior before the bottom was clear of sharp weeds clawing at our bare legs.

"Look, a line of ducks." I pointed as they passed by.

Sean spit out some lake water. "Geese, Natalie, Canada geese."

I looked toward shore. The lifeguard was bent over a computer on his lap. "What if we drown?"

"Two women are swimming out even farther—one's already

gone under." Sean's dry silliness kills me. I laughed loud and long. The lifeguard almost looked up—but didn't.

This was summer. The way it's supposed to be—water and green and a close, pale sky. How it was when I was young.

As we swam back to shore, I noticed the lifeguard had fallen asleep, his chin collapsed on his chest. Even my screaming in half-glee, racing with Sean, passing over the weeds again, did not stir him.

We grabbed our thin white towels, walked off to sit under a silver maple, closed our eyes, and followed the breath for a half hour—all the way in, all the way out, the sun and leaf shadows playing over our bodies.

I was oddly moody walking back down the dirt-and-pebbled path. "Do you feel how soft the air is?" I said a few times. I was trying to get at something.

Two days before, we had flown in from New Mexico, with its sharp, dry light, changing planes in Baltimore, landing in Albany, an hour and a half from this retreat center. I let the late eastern thick season seep into me.

I missed going to my family plot on Long Island. It had been two years since I had bent over the stones of Rose and Sam Edelstein, my grandparents; and Benjamin Goldberg, my zany, adored, difficult father. I'd only had a single visit with my mother's stone, Sylvia Helen Goldberg, beautiful, and dead four and a half years.

I wanted to call my father Papa, the way he called his Russian immigrant father. "Papa, come swim with me. We'll eat chicken sandwiches wrapped in waxed paper on plaid wool blankets, soft and hot from the sand."

How does one deal with the known world when it is swept away?

· · ·

"My purse." I reached for my hip. "It's gone." I looked down. "I left it either at the beach—or at the café before we left. Remember? I got a Popsicle."

I headed up the hill and Sean went to search the lakeshore. Nothing.

We announced it that afternoon to the 150 students. The institute's assistant went to inquire at the lost and found.

"It will show up," someone said.

It didn't until this last morning.

The student who had found it was sly. "You owe me something."

My mind raced. "Come up here." I motioned, catching on.

Sean said, "See if the twenty is still in there."

"You want to know the secret of writing, huh? What I promised? The bounty I offered." She was kneeling next to me now. I was quiet, looking for words. "You know I wrote a 250-page book to answer that question." She didn't budge. "Out in March 2013." My little joke didn't make a dent. I wasn't getting away that glibly. The class was dead still.

I took a leap. I turned to the class. "Why don't you give me the answer? All of you—see what comes from the bottom of your mind. Wait. Let it come to you. Receive it."

These easterners are scruffy, tough, critical, literary. It's their facade. Win their trust and they turn belly-up, like puppies, or cavort like sweet lambs. My tenderness for these students at that moment, as they sat with closed eyes, searching inside themselves for the answer, was so profound I could hardly breathe.

We will never be in this configuration again.

I've taught so much over the last thirty-five years—all over the country—and in France and Italy too. The students come and go, sometimes returning after many years. They seem younger than they used to be. I have to be willing to say good-bye over and over—not hold on to any of them. Freedom to come and go. As my Zen training says, "The door swings both ways."

And yet, some students stay. They take on the practice in their core, show up at every retreat, come consistently every December and August for ten years running. I get to know these students, and a genuine teacher-student relationship—in the old style of Zen, face-to-face—develops.

I wasn't available for this at first. I was in my thirties when my first book came out and still so much a student of my own teacher. I wasn't sure how to handle so much energy coming at me. So I was strict, boundaried—and brittle. But if you managed not to be deflected and came again and again, I softened.

My longtime students used to pull new students aside. "Stay away from her outside the class," they warned. "She's a bitch." But I felt like they would eat me alive.

A long time passed before I realized my own teacher was simply human. When I finally did, I was free—and full of gratitude. The wide gap closed.

At the end of retreats even my most dedicated students forget to thank me. They gush about the cooks, the assistant, even the groundskeepers—and I sit in the circle, holding the emptiness at their backs, and no one notices. I hope for their sake they notice before I die.

It's not unlike our attitude toward our parents. Mostly we don't notice them. And when we are young, it works well that way. They are just there. A friend told me recently that she was driving her sixteen-year-old daughter to yet another ballet class, and right on Berger Street, on the east side of Santa Fe, she had a meltdown. Clutching the steering wheel, she cried, "Amanda, will you ever say you love me? Will you ever say thank you?"

The daughter turned and looked at her as though she were crazy.

My friend said to herself, *Now, Susan, pull yourself together.* Buson has a haiku:

> In the autumn wind,
> I think only
> of my parents

I assume his parents were dead. If his parents were alive when he wrote it, I would be doubly impressed with his meeting life with life when it's happening, right here. But he met his emotion in any case.

"Okay, ready to tell me?" I asked the students.

"Give us another minute," someone called out.

"Ohh-kay."

Lunch will be soon. Then I will drive four hours to the Cape, where I've never been, to do a solo retreat at a cabin in the woods. Recently a good friend died, and another I'd worked with for twenty years had colon cancer.

I thought parents were the big deaths, and once those were over I could relax. No more deaths for twenty years.

Not the case at all.

Recently I admitted I had nothing to write about—the well was dried up. A week alone? I'd made the plan months ago. I was beginning to dread it, even panic. How long had it been since I was totally on my own for a week? At age thirty-three, when I was a young poet, I went to Michael Dennis Browne's cabin in northern Minnesota and wrote for three weeks, living on bananas and chocolate chips.

In two more months I'd begin a yearlong sabbatical. No teaching. I wasn't sure that, at sixty-six, I'd ever teach again.

"Now are you ready?" I asked.

The student next to me nodded. "I found your purse hanging off a slat on the white fence by the lake. I went swimming early this morning, and when I came out, I saw it. I thought then, *What is the true secret for me?*" She clutched her breast and said, "I have to trust myself."

Immediately a few students yelled out their versions: "I have to have courage." "Speak from my heart." "Know myself."

I crinkled my nose and shook my head. "No. No. No. Not even close. It's not about how you feel."

At this point they were beginning to push in on me, getting up from their chairs. "What? What is it?" Hurrah for the determination of easterners.

I mouthed slowly, word upon word: "You. Have. To. Pick. Up. The pen—and write. Just. Write.

"For years, that's all I've been saying. If it's hot out, write in the heat. If it's cold, pull on a sweater and write. Cut through, immediate. Act. You don't have to change a thing. Writing doesn't ask you to be any different from who you are right now. Not better, not more."

They all fell back in their seats. After a long silence, feet, hands, notebooks began to shuffle. It was time to go.

"I'm sorry I didn't see it when I went back," Sean whispered. "I looked and looked."

"You were not meant to see it. She had to find it. It was perfect."

19

Another New Year

I wake up this first bitter-cold day of the New Year, the streets an ice sheet, and recall my dream: Small mice are marching across a flower-wallpapered bedroom with an unmade mattress on the floor, and my friend Sean Murphy sits curled up around his guitar in a wooden chair, weeping that his father never asked him to play, and this New Year's no one did either. I clutch his hand, comforting him, at the same time commanding the cats to catch the mice. No one is listening. The cats do not scare the mice. The mice keep coming.

I lie in bed in my home in Santa Fe with the dream all over my face—the linoleum floor, the woman in the next apartment with bleached-blond hair dropping off her yellow cat, the brick tenements through the window, how very large and empty that dream apartment of mine is.

The night before, at ten o'clock, I had snapped my Yaktrax to the bottom of my snow boots and trudged under a full complement of stars in a black sky to Upaya Zen Center across the road, where seventy of us sat for two hours, then listened at midnight to 108 bells ringing out the year, followed by a short talk by the roshi (my dear friend Joan Halifax) and then tea and cookies in the kitchen.

I ate way too many but insisted this was just what I needed. At the time I meant the cookies, but really it was sitting still in the dark zendo, breathing with others, coming together in this sober way on the last night of the year. More than *deep* or *spiritual* or any of the words one would imagine with a statue of Manjusri—his sword of wisdom slicing through ignorance—on the altar and candles flickering, what I felt was *relief*. To stop at the end of a hectic year that I was trying so hard to rein in, then surrender to, wondering what this human life is all about.

My mind wandered to the actress I had met at the same New Year's Eve sit three years ago. How much I liked her, how she looked both beautiful and tired. I'd heard a few months ago that she had breast cancer. At any age this is bad, but in your seventies—even if you got the best care and survived—it was a big toll on an aging body.

That evening I told her how I loved her Broadway performance.

"Did you really? Why didn't you come backstage afterward to tell me?"

"It never occurred to me." I didn't think you could go backstage. I loved her innocence and insecurity—and that her vulnerability remained after all of her years of fame.

Lying in bed thinking of all the chemo, the visits to doctors, the exhaustion, blood tests, worry, hope, phone calls, antiseptic hospital—"It's about death, isn't it, Nat?" I said to myself. "Either way, no matter what, there is death at the end."

My mind flew back to ten years ago: a sawed-off shotgun at my neck. "Give me your purse." The front door to the apartment building an arm's length away, nine in the evening under the front porch light. I fooled him and gave him my athletic bag instead, clear and unafraid—but on the other side of the door, back in my small rented living room, I was shattered, hysterical, terrified. All weekend I did not leave the apartment, and that Monday morning I had to appear at 5:00 A.M. in front of the Zen teacher I'd come back to the Twin Cities to study with. There was a plan to receive dharma transmission, permission to teach in my old Japanese teacher's lineage. He had died ten years before. I was in my early fifties, still working out his death, thinking that if I was in his teaching lineage he'd be able to meet me on the other side. The silver death plane would land and, voilà—he would be standing at gate 57, waiting for me. It was naive, stupid; I hadn't thought it all through. Deeply entangled, I'd hauled my ass—and my furniture—once again to the upper Midwest in my blind drive to work it out.

And I'm glad I did. One early morning in a clear, ordinary moment I realized I didn't want dharma transmission. I didn't need anything from this teacher in front of me. We were both free: no one could give me my own authority. I always felt great gratitude toward this teacher for the opportunity to discover that.

But that morning, forty-eight hours after being assaulted, all I thought was how I was going to dash to my car across the street, unlock it and get in before another man with a shotgun grabbed me. My imagination was wild with armed young men at every corner at 4:30 A.M., waiting for tender Zen students.

I made it to the car, got the key in the ignition, squeezed out onto the street from between a large Ford and a van, drove down the avenue to the zendo, and entered the small dokusan room. I was off-the-charts shaking, telling the teacher about what had happened three nights earlier.

He listened. "You are afraid of death."

I reeled, then fell through. All the other details dropped away.

My body relaxed. Something made sense, something I could work with.

And now, ten years later on a New Year's morning, I thought about this again. I had gotten hard results from an early-autumn blood test. Not terminal illness, but slowly—and it had probably been happening for a long time—death was making its meandering way through my body. In the last months, though I managed to function well, underneath I was swimming in an abyss and could not find a foothold. I tried to imagine travel, things I'd never done before and wanted to do—I couldn't think of a thing. What did I want to change? Nothing. What did I regret and wished I'd done differently? Usually I'm a great lamenter, but faced with the bold truth of my finite life, I caved in to my past, almost accepting it all.

Then sleepless nights would punctuate my dull submission, tormenting me with failure in all directions. The still night, the click of the clock in the other room, knowing that the next morning I was leaving on a trip, seemed to enhance my despair. All of my life I'd been stalked by extremes, but now the fire burned hotter, fueled by terror. In the past my most reliable elixir had been to continue under all circumstances. But now the biting thought: someday no circumstances will exist.

When my father died, I felt how very close death was; when my mother died, the veil was lifted. The illusion that my parents were a wall, a guard, a boundary between me and the end was over. Death became familial. But when the condition was mine directly, landed in my body, there was nothing vague. The day I heard of my physical condition, a Wednesday, reality opened up, like taking LSD, but this time nobody could come along on my trip.

And yet, it's hard to stay in relation to death. An equal urge arises to race to the bank, to the grocery before it closes. Daily life is so seductive: we believe if we keep moving we can finally catch up, get our bills paid for all time.

We also believe our stories. Everyone does. But where would we be without them? They embrace the full contradictions of our lives.

I remember when I was up in Minnesota, I had to drive through the Zen teacher's hometown to get to Hibbing, where Bob Dylan was raised. I stopped outside the teacher's childhood home, the deep front lawn, the gray clapboard house in the distance. I remembered his telling me about his sister, who became vice president of one of the large airlines and all at once couldn't take the pressure, the success. She moved back to their town on the Iron Range. I thought about how deep the tracks of lineage and pattern and family run.

Death is only half the story. The other half is life, how to navigate in these slippery waters, how to keep the humbling knowledge of our end in sight. We all seem to blow it one way or another, but how important it is to admit our mistakes, not turn our back on anything. It's in the details of what we have done that we can find our liberation.

In the introduction to *Death in the Afternoon,* Hemingway's book about bullfighting in Spain, he writes that he wanted to study death. It's so easy to forget, move away from the heat and honesty of our moments. We need stories to remind us and to mirror our reality. And we need writers to record them.

Leaping

Now we get closer to what I have known
A bare cushion
a steel night
nothing moving but the mountains
and the enormous sky

20

Meeting the Chinese in St. Paul

As a Soto Zen student, I had successfully steered clear of koans for almost my full twenty-five years of practice. They were considered more a part of the fierce Rinzai Zen training and seemed enigmatic and scary. How would I know what my original face was before my parents were born? Koans were meant to stump the student, kick her into another way of thinking—or not thinking—so that she could have insight into the nature of the universe.

My old Soto teacher said, "Soto is more like the not-so-bright, kindly elder uncle." He admired Rinzai and said it was for sharper types.

Despite my reservations, in 1998 I moved up to St. Paul, Minnesota, for two months to dive into koans through the study of *The Book of Serenity,* an ancient Chinese Zen text of one hundred koans (or cases). These depicted situations and dialogues between teacher and student, teacher and teacher, student and student.

Driving in the car through Colorado, Nebraska, Iowa—crossing one state border after another—I repeated to myself, *Yes, I can do it.*

My old friend Phil Willkie and I were going to trade homes from mid-October through mid-December. We didn't know who was getting the better deal. I would live in his three-bedroom, fourth-floor walk-up flat on Mackubin in St. Paul, and he would inhabit my solar beer-can and tire house on the mesa, six miles outside of Taos.

Phil's apartment was replete with photos of his family, including one of his grandfather Wendell Willkie, the 1940 contender for the presidency against FDR, and another of an aunt sitting in the backseat of a convertible with Dwight Eisenhower. A former boyfriend of Phil's lived in the back bedroom. He, too, was studying Zen at the time. At night we'd often share a simple dinner of steamed broccoli and rice. He was a modest fellow, saving all plastic yogurt containers and calling them his fine Tupperware collection. We knew each other from years before, when he and Phil visited me in the Southwest.

During the day, I had little else to do but wrestle with these Chinese ancestors who embodied the koans.

Luoshan runs into Shishuang and asks: "When arising and vanishing go on unceasingly, what then?"

A perfectly good question, if you were thinking about the nature of the universe.

We often ask, "What should I do with my life?" Usually it's asked in despair. *I'm lost; help me.* We want a concrete answer: *Become a dentist and everything will be all right.* But there is a deeper cry in the question. *How should I live, knowing the world is a confusing place?*

Shishuang replied: "You must be cold ashes, a dead tree, one thought for ten thousand years, box and lid joining, pure and spotlessly clear."

Luoshan didn't get it. Too complicated an answer. He only became more confused trying to figure it out.

So he went seeking Yantou and asked his question again. "When arising and vanishing go on unceasingly, what then?"

Yantou shouted and then said, "Whose arising and vanishing is it?"

Maybe the shout would have been enough.

Imagine that you're an earnest student going from teacher to teacher, saying, "Please clarify this," and one of the renowned, respected ones screams in your face. Maybe then you'd step back and see yourself. But Yantou offers more than his shout. He asks, *Who are you that is experiencing this coming and going?* This time Luoshan is enfolded into his own question. Engulfed in nonseparation, he wakes up.

I understood what was happening to Luoshan. But my understanding wasn't good enough. The koan wouldn't come alive until I demonstrated that understanding.

There is an old adage in writing: Don't tell but show. I could tell you what happened in the koan, but to show it, I had to become Luoshan and exhibit his—and my—insight. That's how I would pay true homage to the lineage of old Chinese practitioners I'd come to love—by making their work and effort alive in me and vital right now.

To stay Natalie Goldberg from Brooklyn with her usual collection of needs and desires, pains and complaints, wouldn't work. Becoming some idea of Chinese—or Japanese—wouldn't work either. These koans might come through a particular culture, but what they are aiming at is the core of human nature: Who are we really? What is this life about?

I had to learn to become a fool, a barbarian—or the moon, a lamppost, a fallen leaf—to answer the questions. But

I also couldn't get stuck—not even as a single perfect plum blossom.

My mind had to become greased in its skull, a pearl rolling in a silver bowl. No settling; no abiding; no fixed residence. The koan mind does not dwell; instead it is alive—and empty—like a dust mote in a ray of sun. I had to let go, see fresh, like a blind donkey. Tell me, how can something sightless see?

I paced St. Paul's streets, past Scott Fitzgerald's old home on Summit, the vast houses on Crocus Hill, the River Gallery, the Great Harvest Bread Company. I crossed the bridge over the Mississippi, reveling in the long, slow display of burned leaves that marked the coming of the dark season. I wanted to know who these Chinese brothers—and the occasional Chinese sister, such as Iron-Grinder Lui, the woman of Taishan, and the tea cake seller—were. I was used to studying Western literature, full of elaborate stories, subplots, metaphors, and flashbacks. These Chinese tales were so digested that only a few lines were enough.

Leaning over our supper plates one evening, Phil's old boyfriend from the back room beseeched me, "So, Aunt Natalie, tell me a bedtime koan before we drop off." It was his second year of practice, and his early enthusiasm met my old determination.

I lunged into the koan about Luoshan. I described the rough road, the jagged mountain where I imagined the interchange had taken place. I fleshed out the two men's ragged dress, their recent meal—"For sure, it was not hot dogs on a bun." I wanted to plant a deep impression in my faux nephew's mind so he would never forget these crazy wild ancestors. I made faces with lips turned out, eyes raised to the ceiling; I howled, groaned, drooled, clawed at Yantou. I demanded a response to rising and vanishing.

We both went to bed tired and giddy that night—then woke at 4:30 A.M. and drove the mile and a half to the zendo.

Later that morning, I unfolded on my bedroom floor a glossy map of the whole Zen lineage from 532 C.E. to 1260 C.E. I knelt over it, running my finger from Matsu to Pai-Chang to Kuei-shan. These were all characters in the *Book of Serenity*. I relished the link of teacher and student and how the student became the teacher in the next generation.

Below all the dates and Chinese names was a drawing of an immense fork-tongued dragon sprouting out of the clouds. He was a feral force in the orderly map of connections.

The original *Book of Serenity* was lost when it was first compiled by Wansong in northern China but was reconstructed by him at the urging of one of his disciples, Yelü Chucai. He was one of a group of Chinese statesmen who were desperate to save their provinces from destruction by the ravaging army of Genghis Khan, and they wanted to study the text as a way to illuminate their minds and come up with a fresh solution. Through their work they eventually softened the harshness of the Mongol ruler.

Studying these cases brings one more fully and deeply into the structures that underlie conventional life. The cases were not created to help people disappear into a mist high on a mountain. The terrible truth, which is rarely mentioned, is that meditation doesn't directly lead us to some vaporous, glaze-eyed peace. It drops us right into the personal meat of human suffering. No distant, abstract idea of distress. Instead we get to taste the bitter pain between our own twin eyes. With practice we settle right down into the barbed wire nest, and this changes us. Working with koans creates a bigger heart; a tender, more close existence; a deeper seeing.

. . .

Near the end of November, I turned to page 108, case 25. "Rhinoceros Fan" was the title. My mind froze.

That's my usual tactic: when anything new comes along, brake, clutch, stop dead.

What do I know about a rhinoceros? Aren't they African? I later found out that China did have rhinos, and that their horns were carved into fans.

What stumped me even more was the juxtaposition of those two words: *rhinoceros,* that huge, forceful animal, probably as close to a dinosaur as we are going to find now on Earth, placed beside the word *fan,* something light, used to create a breeze to refresh court ladies or southern belles.

I moved on from the title to the actual case.

> One day Yanguan called to his attendant, "Bring me the rhinoceros fan."
> The attendant said, "The fan is broken."
> Yanguan said, "If the fan is broken, then bring me back the rhinoceros!"
> The attendant had no reply.
> Zifu drew a circle and wrote the word *rhino* inside it.

Yanguan was an illustrious disciple of Matsu. After his teacher's death, he wandered until he became the abbot of Fayao Temple. This was a monastery. The attendant was not paid staff but Yanguan's student. As an attendant, the student had the great opportunity of extra time with his teacher.

In this particular story, the student was anonymous. All the better; he could be any of us—John or Sue or Sally, you or me.

I was not sure who Zifu was. I would look him up later. But for now I'd stay with the teacher-and-student interaction.

More than likely, their interchange takes place in a quiet

moment, when Yanguan has a little time to put his attention on this monk. He's going to test him, poke him—*Are you there?* Yanguan and the attendant are in kinship. They had both probably lived in the monastery for many years, but Yanguan can't turn around to the attendant and say something simple like, "Do you love me?" or "Are you happy here?" Instead there is decorum. One person is made the attendant, the other the Zen master. Of course, one has been practicing longer than the other. (Out of time we create hierarchy, levels, positions. In the large space of this true *Book of Serenity*, we eventually let go of criteria, but we also play along.)

So Yanguan asks for a fan. The fan is the excuse for an exchange, though it could also have been one of those unbearable hot summer days. *Bring me some relief. Where's the fan?*

The attendant replies that the fan is broken.

He can't find another one? I'm thinking. *What was going on here?*

That evening, after I read this case, I couldn't sleep. I tossed and turned.

The night became deep and endless. My mind wandered over much terrain: a particular apple orchard, a young boy who died. I remembered an old friendship I once had. This line ran through my head: *The relationship is broken.*

Broken! I sat up in bed. That is the word the attendant used.

I jumped up, ran to the shelf, opened the book. I took a leap: the attendant was saying he himself was broken, even if he referred to a fan. He was the fan.

But that doesn't stop Yanguan, his teacher. Hell, if the fan—the product—was shattered, then bring back the whole rhinoceros. What a stunning concept! If the paper is torn, bring the enormous tree into the living room.

Yanguan was asking this of his student (and of us): take a tremendous step—not forward, but backward—into your essential nature. Manifest your original face. Don't get stuck on something broken—a heart, a wish. Become the rhinoceros—reveal your full self, go to the source, nothing hidden.

And this is what I loved the most: "The attendant had no reply." What do we do when a rhino is charging us, when a bear of a teacher is storming us? Run for our lives.

In no other case that I had studied so far was there such an abrupt stop. No action, nothing. The attendant had already given his all when he said the fan was broken, when he revealed he was not whole.

It's a naked thing to show that we are fractured, that we do not have it all together. Broken all the way through to the bottom. What freedom that is, to be what we are in the moment, even if it's unacceptable. Then we are already the rhinoceros.

Think about it: We are always doing a dance—*I'm good; I'm bad; I'm this; I'm that.* Rather than the truth: *I don't know who I am.* Instead we scurry to figure it out. We write another book, buy another blouse. We exhaust ourselves.

Imagine the freedom to let it be, this not knowing. How vulnerable.

This is why I love the attendant. He said who he was—a broken man, a shattered fan, derived from the concentrated point of a fierce beast. When his teacher asked for more, the monk didn't do a jig to win him over. There was no more. Usually we will do anything to cover up a reality so naked.

I know the relief, and ensuing shame or terror, of making that kind of simple statement. When I was in the middle of a divorce, I visited my parents in Florida. My father was on the first day of a new diet. He was looking forward to dinner. We were going out to a steak house for the early bird special. My father made fun of my huarache sandals when I stepped out of the bedroom, ready to go.

"What are those, horse hooves?"

I was touchy and tired of his put-downs. I twirled around and marched back into the bedroom. "I'm leaving," I screamed. I threw clothes into a suitcase, charged out the front door and onto the nearby turnpike.

I was walking on the divider line, headed for the airport fifteen miles away. A car pulled up beside me and drove the speed of my walking pace. I looked straight ahead.

My father rolled down his window. "Nat."

I burst out crying.

"Wait, stay here, I'll go get your mother. Do you promise not to move?"

I nodded, leaning against the guardrail.

Moments later my parents pulled up together. My mother ran out of the car. "Natli, what's the matter?"

I uttered three words: "I am lost." I had no energy for a cover-up. Those words came from my core.

Everything halted. My mother stood with her hands at her sides. My father looked straight ahead, his face frozen, his arm hanging over the door of the car.

Nothing was to be done. It was a huge, unbearable opening between us.

My parents became embarrassed. So was I. We'd never been so naked with each other.

After a long, excruciating time, my father's head turned. "Now can we go eat? I'm starving."

• • •

The monk did not have this distraction. No restaurant for him. My experience was that the monk stood his ground for all time. He did not reply after he revealed his naked face.

But like the rabbis making commentary on the Torah, later Zen teachers responded to koans. In this case, they disagreed about the monk's state of mind. Maybe the attendant in his silence had emptied his depths, and the rhinoceros, the source, stood there radiantly, painfully alive in his no reply. Or maybe he was just dumbfounded, petrified, thinking, *What should I do now in front of my teacher?*

In the next sentence, Zifu draws a circle and writes the word *rhino* inside it. I imagine he picked up a nearby stick and drew the circle in the dirt or in the air and wrote the Chinese character boldly in the center.

I found out later that Zifu was himself a Zen master—one who lived at least a hundred years after the interchange between Yanguan and the monk. Sitting in his monastery, Zifu heard the situation and plunged in. His dust circle was a stamp of approval. His response radiated back through a century and screams forward to us now.

Attendant, I see you! Zifu called out.

Yes, this exchange between student and teacher is complete; nothing is left out. Even if the attendant might have been immobilized rather than inexpressively present, Zifu catches the whole interchange and brings it to completion, enlightening the attendant, the rhino, the teacher, and folding us all into the great circle.

I spent the entire autumn of my fiftieth year roaming through these Chinese minds. I began to see everything as a koan. On the evening news it was reported that a bread loaf burned in someone's kitchen in Blue Earth and the house went down in flames. Everything was now related. The house, the bread, the town in southern Minnesota, presented a koan. How could I step into those flames and burn too? Life became a revolving story. No matter from what age or country, it met me where I was.

I watched my friend Wendy, an old practitioner and the gardener for twenty years at Green Gulch, a Zen farm outside San Francisco, answer questions after a reading from her book, *Gardening at the Dragon's Gate.*

"How big is your garden?" one of my students asked.

Wendy was struck silent for a full minute. The audience fidgeted in their seats. I realized what was happening.

I leaned over. "Wendy, this is not a koan—she's not challenging your whole being. She just wants to know in feet the area you garden."

Wendy snapped back. "Many feet are cultivated." Then she went on to speak of once putting a dead deer in the compost heap, and a month later nothing was left but hooves and bones.

In the *Book of Serenity* Guishan asks Yangshan, *Where do you come from?* and Yangshan replies, *The fields.* There are many fields to come from—playing fields, plowing fields, the upper or lower field, or the dharma field spread out before us.

Soon after I returned home to Taos, I had a week of teaching with my good friend Rob Wilder. He is sharp and has a generous heart. Little goes by him. We sat together at dinner the second night of the workshop. I was eager to share where I had been. I told him about koans; then I told him about the last one I worked on. I laid out the case, how I entered it, what I understood. He listened intently, the way only a writer can from years of developing an attunement to story and sound. He nodded often. I felt encouraged.

I went to bed that night happy. I had been afraid, coming home from St. Paul, that no one would understand where I had been.

The next morning was a silent breakfast. Almost everyone had cleared out of the dining room when Rob sidled up next to me. "Nat," he said in a low voice, "I was thinking how amazing it is. We can know each other so well. We can be such good friends, and I had no idea what you were talking about last night."

My head snapped back. *What's going on here? The fan of our communication is fractured?*

A student walked in and we shut up.

I gulped down some water to swallow the ball of cornflakes that sat in my mouth. I felt lonely, on the brink of isolation.

Suddenly something in front of my eyes shattered. The rhino emerged, glistening.

I abruptly started to laugh, big eruptions through my entire body. This was one whole world. Rob Wilder was my relation. We had plunged right into the lineage together. No one left out. His not understanding was part of it. The water glass, the spoon, the flowers in the vase, all glimmered and shook. Who was laughing? Hours melted in my hand. The walls of the building dissolved.

Everyone and no one lifted the spoon to take the next bite of cereal.

21

First Edition

My first semester in college, two months away from home, I had a blind date with a young man—a boy really, nineteen, a sophomore at a college two hours south. University of Virginia. 1966. I stood in the lobby of Thurston Hall, waiting for him.

His name was Robbie Rosen. He was from Charleston, South Carolina. A Jew who loved literature the way I did. We began talking immediately about *The Brothers Karamazov*. Thin, wiry, energetic, he'd begun a magazine down there, with JFK on the cover of its first issue. I can't say I fell in love; that has too much weight and density. Instead I'd found someone with passion.

Robbie was going to be a writer; he loved his hometown; and he had a sense of place. "The Ashley and Cooper Rivers wrap around the city and meet in the Atlantic." I imagined the distant sprawl and cascade of water. He talked about Charleston all the time, and I knew even then that no matter where this person wandered, he would end up where he began. He had no choice. His love was deep and rooted.

Forty years later, Robbie Rosen is still vivid for me. Something in him knew who he was, where he came from. No other person I met during college was as memorable. The rest of us could have scattered to the moon—or New Jersey, Boston, the Big Apple—by luck or chance. We had no innate connection anywhere.

I was mad for poetry and novels, but who was I? My father owned a bar. My mother shopped. We had no books in our house. What we read in English class was written by white men, often dead, from across the ocean. Their experience was not mine. I caught colds, sneezed in my grandmother's chicken soup, opened and closed the refrigerator, bought chewing gum. I wasn't worthy of literature. I never even dreamed of pen in hand and suffered no rough angst. So I remembered Robbie for the two things that would grow in me—writing and place.

One afternoon the phone rang in my adobe in New Mexico. A woman named Carolyn from the Sophia Institute on Society Street in Charleston wanted me there to teach.

Before this request, I'd found the South impossible to penetrate. No one, in my twenty-five years since *Writing Down the Bones* had been published, had ever invited me to the South. On my own I'd visited Oxford, Mississippi, where the great store Square Books had none of mine. The new lineage of writing practice that I'd sprung, based on two thousand years of watching the mind, of making writing a practice, like tennis, running, chess, or tea ceremony, did not interest the South. It was drenched in its own weighty, azalea-soaked history. But even more than my abiding curiosity about southern writers was the single question I asked on the phone: "Do you know Robbie Rosen?"

This was not what she expected. "Why, yes," she drawled out. "He's an attorney in town, a friend of the institute. His wife is in a book club with me."

"I used to date him in college—only for a few months."

"Well, we'll have to get you together with Robert."

The following January I fly across the country.

I'm at the end of a flu, and after the weekend I'll go down to Florida to try to organize my mother's house. She's been dead a year, and a gray sadness still hangs around me.

Carolyn picks me up at the airport and tells me that a small gathering at Robbie's house has been organized for the next night. He'd seen a pile of my books, different titles, on a table at Barnes and Noble a year back and realized it was the same Natalie Goldberg he knew. She adds, "But I don't think he bought or read any of them."

In the brisk early evening, as we pull away from the airport in her car, I ask this woman I'd just met, "So tell me, what's he like now? I don't want to see him and have shock on my face. He must be gray. Is he still skinny and wiry? Tell me, does he still have that adorable nose?"

She bursts out laughing. "Only a lover would notice something like that. I never considered his nose."

I look out at the close dark and vaguely remember that his mother was already dead when I met him. Something about being beautiful and crazy. It didn't mean anything to me then. But now I know the pain of family relations.

Carolyn tells me he has a law firm with his wife; they have three children; he wrote a book about Jews in Charleston, another about "some kind of history."

Oh, good, he's been writing, I think.

Back then, when he heard I was from New York, he wanted to visit at Christmas. New York meant nothing to him except the city. What a surprise for him to end up for seven days an hour away in a split-level development on the Nassau/Suffolk border on Long Island. We went into Manhattan only once, when my father loaned us his tan Buick to drive in to the Big Apple and meet some of Robbie's friends from Larchmont, a wealthy and sophisticated suburb.

After that vacation was over, I returned to college and never heard from him again. I knew I wouldn't—I'd been dumped. He sent my parents a thank-you gift, an ashtray.

But back then, it was easy to move on.

Now I was a writer, coming to Charleston, a place I'd heard so much about but had never been to. I felt good in my success, happy that this little nothing from the suburbs, who didn't even dare wish to be a writer, had climbed through her haze and managed to speak—and some people had listened.

The night before I arrived, Carolyn had called a woman from Sullivan's Island to drive in for the party at Robert's (I found out no one called him Robbie). Three years earlier, she'd come to study with me in Taos and was working on a novel. "Oh, I wish I could, but we're leaving for Panama early the next day and we have to pack."

"So sorry you can't make it. The gathering is at Robert Rosen's."

"Robert Rosen? What does he have to do with Natalie?"

"She dated him in college."

"No!" A long pause. "I'll be there."

We pull up to a large historical house with a circular drive-way, heavy foliage, and a wraparound veranda. A man comes to the door. It has to be him. The slightly curly hair—it used to be a shock of chocolate-red curls. He's wearing a bow tie. "Robbie?"

We are happy to see each other, and the four of us—including Carolyn and her husband, Hank—stand awkwardly, filling the vestibule so no one else can pass. Out of the corner of my eye I see ornate wallpaper and wood floors. I want to stare and touch. This is a life in America so different from mine in the Southwest.

Robert's wife is out of town, but his daughter, in her early twenties, is across a small sitting room. Though she is blond, with straight hair, she looks more like the Robbie of my memory. His skin is paler now, with no trace of that slight spray of freckles.

The present fades. The unimaginable ages of eighteen and nineteen step forward like real beings and stand beside us. Who we were then is vivid, almost luminous. I feel the fullness of how my life was forty years ago.

Robert does not remember coming to my family's house—or dropping me. He carries no memory at all of my mother and father. But I do, and I link a small part of them with him. When your parents are dead, anyone who passed time with them has a connection to you. For that I feel suddenly happy.

Connie, my writing student, comes through the door. Robert introduces us and says, "This is my former psychiatrist. She saved my marriage. She told me to do everything my wife wants."

My mouth hangs open. While she studied with me, he was doing therapy with her across the country?

She taps him in the stomach. "That isn't what I said."

He takes me into an adjoining room full of rare out-of-print hardbacks and shows me the books he's written, centered on the South, Jews, and Charleston, including *The Jewish Confederates, A Short History of Charleston,* and a weighty tome *Saving the Jews: Franklin D. Roosevelt and the Holocaust,* correcting the image of FDR's anti-Semitism.

Five of us—my two hosts, Carolyn and Hank, Robbie, his daughter, and I—go to the Hominy Grill for dinner after the reception. Carolyn maneuvers it so Robbie and I sit together and have a little time to talk. They encourage me to order shrimp with grits.

He tells me he was married before to a New Yorker who couldn't bear living in the South, and then changes the subject to a meeting where he knew the people were anti-Semites. He let them have it. His daughter rolls her eyes, but it's evident she adores him. I notice she has the nose I was looking for on Robbie. She says, "He voted for Bush in the last election."

I screech, "You couldn't have. You, Robbie Rosen!"

His daughter leans across the table. "Even my mother didn't, and she usually would." Her face brightens. "So they canceled each other out."

He tells me, "Doing research for the FDR book, you wouldn't believe what I read. They had to plan all of those deaths." He shakes his head and he grimaces. "So gruesome. It was all thought out. You can't imagine. Bush is for Israel."

I ask him if he knew John Lewis. I have all of my longtime students read *Walking in the Wind,* his memoir of the civil rights movement.

He says Lewis has been to his house.

He gives me *Saving the Jews* and I carry it down to Florida. In between sorting my mother's old trousseau silk nightgowns she'd bought sixty years ago at Macy's and the old rusted tools in the garage, I page through his book. Though its heft is imposing, the text is not. It's clear, engagingly written, not only for historians but for general readers. He wants us to understand. With more than a hundred pages of bibliography, I conclude he spent years in research. I feel proud of him.

Three months later, buds cracking through the April trees in

New Mexico, I receive a weighty overnight package from Fed Ex. My heart sinks. It's obviously another request for a cover blurb. I open it.

Inside is a first edition hardback of John Lewis's book. And Lewis has signed it and written, "Thank you for all of your good work. Keep the faith." I hug it to my chest.

22

A Time of No Place

I have so many good memories—swimming in the Atlantic as a young girl; sleeping under the stars by the Chama River in New Mexico; eating cherry pie with my ninety-year-old mother at Hamburger Heaven in Palm Beach, Florida; the gray-brown deer, considered sacred, that ripped the map out of my friend's hand in Kyoto; eating green tea ice cream out of a Dixie cup in front of the gates to Eiheiji Monastery, deep in the mountains outside Fukui—yet it's none of these that I recall this early January morning. What halts me like a shot of cold electricity is the stunning thought of the six months I spent miserably unhappy in Palo Alto, California, six years previously, at the beginning of this century.

I had gone straight to California from St. Paul, where I'd practiced for a year and a half with my old Zen teacher's priest. Eventually I was supposed to enter the ancient lineage myself, but that all went awry. I began to trust neither my intentions nor my interactions with the teacher. I found myself spending more of my days at a café than in the zendo. In the evenings I retired to the small apartment I lived in, looking out through my second-floor windows at the green leaves of maples and elms, and in winter through their barren branches. Spring brought the yellow neon skies and 2:00 A.M. downpours. I painted huge abstracts: "Searching for the Moon," "Eye of the Storm," "Inside the Mountain," and "Walking in Ravines."

Something strange and powerful was happening to me up there in the North, but I couldn't recognize it. I went there looking for formal Zen transmission and left disappointed, with only one wish: I wanted more time on the second floor among the trees.

With this ache and confused longing that began in St. Paul, I moved to Palo Alto. My father had recently died, and my mother was alone on the East Coast. I worried about her. We'd been strangers for so long; now she was an old woman who needed me, and instead of being with her, I was moving to the other side of the country.

I probably shouldn't have gone to the Golden State, but I had promised I would. My partner was living in the heart of Silicon Valley, running a small software start-up she and her friend from Sun Microsystems had created. Until then the computer world had passed me by—I'd put off using e-mail until my early fifties. But in Minnesota I was lost—stripped of what I thought I wanted—and one place seemed as good as another.

I stopped home in New Mexico for the Christmas holidays, where I came down with a whopping flu that would not go away, and drove across Arizona with my nose stuffed, eyes watery, and a chest that felt as if I were transporting the weight of the queen's jewels.

In Palo Alto we lived in a tiny, three-room apartment for $2,400 a month. Yes, it was that expensive. A Meyer lemon tree was out back. I made sure to use the fruit—I made gallons of lemonade, lemon pie, lemon soup. Longs Drugs on University

Avenue was the only whiff I had that this place had once been a locale of some simple dignity, drenched in sun with orchards nearby. The lettering on the outside was an old script, and the aisles were lazy and sloppy.

A week into the cramped living arrangements, I took a slow walk one early morning, still sick, thinking maybe we could find a junky fixer-upper nearby. Surely, for the rent we were paying we could own a little house. And behold! Down the block I spied a yellow stucco with a FOR SALE sign. With its twisted wires jutting out of sockets over the sidewalk and its torn-down awnings, this sad, modest fellow must be aching for love. I jotted down the realtor's phone number.

"I'm asking about that rat's nest on Cowper," I said, breathing thickly into the phone, my nose still bountifully stuffed.

"Yes, that property is three million."

The receiver dangled from my hand. I could hear the snap of her cell phone closing. She isn't ashamed to tell me that? I knew I was in strange territory.

Standing in our narrow bedroom, staring blankly ahead, I was jarred by a whirring sound on the street. I tried to ignore it— and when finally I couldn't, I went out to look. A young man was holding the handle to a vibrating motor connected to an extended nozzle pointed at the sidewalk, the nose of which was chasing a single red leaf.

I marched over and motioned vigorously for the man to switch it off. I bent down, grabbed the leaf with my right hand, ceremoniously walked it to the curb and dropped it in the street.

"Use a rake. It's a fine tool." I motioned how to use one. "You're wasting precious oil reserves."

The man was confused. He didn't understand.

"No más," I declared, and crossed my arms. Then, wanting

to make sure the point was made, I did the arrogant thing unilingual Americans do. I repeated myself, slowly, enunciating my words about the rake.

He turned his back on me, blasted his machine again, and chased another solitary leaf.

I whipped around and stomped back into my scrawny apartment. I heard blowers starting up all down the block. What happened to the monk in a mist raking the monastery garden?

At night, when my partner returned, I asked her how it was going. Did the engineers come up with a salable product?

She shrugged her shoulders. "Who knows? I barely see them. They arrive at three in the afternoon and eat doughnuts, preferably with pink icing. They work till the early-morning hours, lost in cyberspace."

I thought of Max, whom I'd met in Cambridge three years earlier. I had seen him intently writing in a notebook at the next table in a restaurant. "Journaling?" I asked.

He looked over. "In a sense. I keep a math notebook. I think mathematically."

"You mean like I might write, 'Today I am grouchy,' but you would write, 'Two plus two is equivalent to eight'?"

"Sort of."

I couldn't leave this alone. I bent over and whispered across his table, "Eight minus three is five."

He gave me a short snort. I threw out everything I could recall from algebra and geometry. I even mentioned Euclid.

He rescued me just as I was about to recite the multiplication tables. "I went to MIT and have a PhD in math."

"May I treat you to a croissant?" Anyone hovering over the slimness of numbers must need sustenance.

He told me about his dissertation, which was almost all equations, though it had jokes on pages 45 and 67.

"So there's personality in math?"

"Sure. My adviser had a Nobel Prize. When he'd pull out his file cabinet drawer, the papers he'd written would swing, balanced in their folders. All of his work condensed on a few pages. Only three people in the world could read his last theorems. Extreme elegance."

I couldn't contain myself. I raised a single finger. "Everything in this, huh?"

He snorted again, but this time he smiled.

My Zen life had been simple. One ring of a bell, one breath, a single candle on the altar, a moment of still peace inside.

But I'd thrown that all out. In another single moment in the zendo in St. Paul, I had seen through all of my cranky desire. Dharma transmission was another way for me to try to secure myself, make myself solid in this transitory world. Nope. I decided to dump myself out into the vast unknown with only a pen, a notebook, and thirty years of sitting practice under my ever-widening belt.

As my father would say, that and a dime will buy you a cup of coffee.

Now here I was with young programmers who ate pink icing, and my future was dependent on them. Would we ever leave this expensive hovel?

Slowly I regained my health and walked the dense streets. March in California—no one tells you this—is the most gorgeous of all months. Everything is blooming and opulent. After living so many years in arid New Mexico, how would I take it in? Just one branch of one bush—and there were often hundreds in one yard—held eighteen perfect flowers. The pinks, the reds, the yellows. What could root me in this abundance? What had happened to my America, to the small, empty towns I loved?

I wanted to liberate my little yellow stucco house and its patch of bare yard, the only place in town where weeds were allowed to grow. Mornings I'd sit on its cracked asphalt patio; I was certain no one would buy this house under the cool shade of a hawthorn.

Eventually I found another refuge, the huge live oaks and white oaks, some of them three hundred years old, looming in yards and bursting out of the concrete sidewalks. All of them alive before this town was here. I became friends with eight of them and visited daily, begging for answers. *What am I doing in this sanitary white place?*

My deepest connection was with an oak that dwarfed a two-story Tudor house on Coleridge. How I loved that the street had the name of a writer. The oak's roots were so big it dominated the lawn. No human could own this wild animal of a tree—or plant flowers around it. Flowers needed surface water, but this white oak, reaching the height of at least a five-story Manhattan building, was drinking from sources deep and unknown, forgotten aquifers way below the earth's surface. Trees of this nature that were watered were known to burst, exploding rooftops and building structures.

One day I knocked on the door of the house. A blond woman with a young child hiding in her skirts opened it.

"I wonder if it's okay that I hang out here a bit sometimes? I've fallen in love with your tree."

"Tree?" she asked with an accent. I could see past the door front. They'd just moved in.

"That one," I pointed. I wanted her, too, to love it. Why else could she have bought the house? The mighty branches extended over the entire yard and out into the street.

She glanced at it. "Oh, yes, it cost a lot when we had it pruned. Sure, it's fine," she said, and shut the door.

Untold money was made during the nineties. Couples in their twenties were suddenly millionaires many times over. The category of billionaire came into being. I knew this owner was part of the phenomenon. Stunned by the sudden wealth, she had no time left to notice the tree. I worried for these people, but I was in my fifties, old enough to worship the great oak. I would do it for all of them.

Before I became a full-time writer, I was a teacher. My last teaching job was with twenty-five fifth- and sixth-graders in a private school. I'd never taught a whole group of white, well-to-do kids before. My specialty was ragtag, sometimes hungry, inner-city kids. I developed writing practice with these young students. Rudely honest and still connected to community and families, however broken, these Chippewa and African American students gave me fresh insights into the writing mind.

But the ten-, eleven-, and twelve-year-olds in this private setting were a phenomenon I'd never encountered before. They came to school well dressed, with too many snacks, but as soon as they were dropped off, all hell broke loose. I was afraid they'd kill each other—or at least break a few arms, legs, and pelvic bones.

"Quick, without thinking, write what your mother was wearing this morning," I said to them in early September.

Most kids don't notice their mothers that much, but their responses gave me some insight.

My mother is in Switzerland. She left two weeks ago, wrote one thin boy. *I haven't seen her in a long time.*

My stepmother was making me breakfast. I hate her. She's a lousy cook. I poured Coke on my cereal, penned a redheaded fifth grader.

I understood that, in these families, material goods replaced human attention, guidance, and touch. Each day I watched these kids take out their frustration and isolation on each other. The wealth served to create loneliness.

I sensed this same vacancy in the quaint, expensive streets that I walked in Palo Alto. Soul was missing; only commerce was left.

Yet when I attended a luncheon celebrating a big investment in my partner's company by a venture capitalist, I was surprised to meet the software engineers, who turned out to be fresh, idealistic, and enthusiastic. They said things we used to say as hippies, only they substituted the word *technology* for the word *love*. "This technology program will change the world, will make it a better place," intoned one young man.

I tried to find some common ground for sharing. Zen? Literature? Writing? These topics got me nowhere. I dropped them and finally just listened. The short-haired blond in a striped polo on my right told me about his love of waves and how he had followed the surf all over the world. The one across the table in a yellow T-shirt and thick glasses spoke of the traditional Korean wedding he would have in six months. He had met his fiancée five weeks earlier in LA. The others teased him, but they were all going to attend the ceremonies.

I tried to ask what they were developing for the company, but no one could tell me. It wasn't a secret, they said. It was just that they hadn't gotten far enough.

I was no computer genius, but I didn't quite believe them, even though I knew they weren't lying. I feared a rootlessness at the core of all of this research.

In truth, I was disappointed that all of this technology was discovered in my lifetime. It seemed to make time busier, more complicated, as if the functions of the mind, the beat of thought I'd come to depend on for my years of sitting and writing practice, no longer applied. I understood how the brain made poetic leaps, how it could juxtapose seemingly dissimilar objects, people, rivers, fruit, how you could reach into the center of the source and discover a vast emptiness that was full and abundant. But the rhythm of the minds partaking of this Caribbean meal felt jagged, even severed in some places, as though natural mind waves had been broken. Some neuron had gone astray from staring for so long at computer screens. All over this heart of Silicon Valley, I sensed some human channel burned out.

In the afternoons I took long walks along a creek that wound between Palo Alto and Menlo Park. I sat on a stone bench to meditate as whole families biked by and couples jogged. From a house across the way I could hear someone practicing the cello. The person was a good musician. These were not beginning chords. I wanted to knock on the door. *Take me in,* I'd demand.

Eventually I found an old Chinese restaurant that had let time pass by. The food was good and not fancy. Its gray walls became my refuge. The waiter recognized me each time I came and knew what I would order: shrimp fried rice. Two dollars more for extra shrimp. I sat in the booth at the back. I felt transported out of sunlit, jazzy California to an old place on Cedar Avenue in Minneapolis. Something ordinary and comforting.

My partner and I were growing distant from each other. Where had she brought me? More important, where had I brought myself?

My source of inspiration had been grounded in a solid, rather unquestioning connection to Zen practice. But back in St. Paul the lineage had crumbled for me. I was in the midst of writing a book about betrayal and failure, about the indiscretions of my teacher. A lot of people I knew didn't want me to write this book. I was on my own. How could I tell anyone what was happening? I was falling backward off the diving board.

One noon I found myself on my knees under the tall eucalyptuses on the Stanford campus.

I wanted to hear an epiphany, some grand realization to give meaning and relief. But no understanding shot through my cells to rectify my birth, my family of origin, the life I was living.

I continued to write my book, to have sleepless nights, to feel biologically out of sync with this new cutting-edge world.

In June, six months after I arrived, I left, driving out through the Sierras, across Utah, dropping down to New Mexico. I remember staying overnight in a barren motel on the California border, sobbing late into the early morning. Nothing was the way I thought. Not a single thing was the way I wanted it.

As I descended into the northwest corner of New Mexico, a single lane of traffic piled up for miles. On all sides was open sage flatland. Nothing broke the horizon. My car inched along. A deep gray began to enfold us. The sky was no longer sky—the smoke from fires hundreds of miles away, burning up thousands of acres of Arizona forest, was coming our way. The air was unbreathable, filled with a suffocating fog. I could almost hear the high-pitched crack of ponderosas exploding in the extreme heat.

All that summer, that dismal cloud hung over Taos. Hands, faces, tables, chairs were gritty from ash. It was also the second year of a severe drought. I put out pans of water for the jackrabbits that usually shot across the mesa, but now even they were drooping. Several times a day I applied lip balm.

I spoke to my partner long distance. The bombing of the Twin Towers wasn't even a year old. Her company was merging with an older company. It was happening because the venture capitalists were skittish after the terrorist attack. It felt like the beginning of worlds being shattered.

· · ·

So why, six years later, leaning over the sink, brushing my teeth in a winter month, do those strange streets in another state call me? Why do they feel so strong that I ache to be back? I can see the library down the block with the English ivy at the entrance-way; the low, white concrete benches; the librarian who allowed me only fifteen minutes at the public computers. I can feel the air conditioner blowing, much too cold.

In Palo Alto I began learning to say good-bye. Layer by layer I was pulling off the old protections. Nowhere could I find a foothold to drag myself away to some safe cave. Everywhere I turned was confusion and suffering, inside me and outside me. No difference. I was saying good-bye to all of my old recourses—I could name a dozen right off the top—from just feeling the pain, from settling down into its scratchy nest. Finally there was nowhere to go, no more hiding place, not even Zen.

This was groundlessness, no abiding. Supposedly a good thing in Zen practice, where you finally unhinge, admit you know nothing, surrender to the vast unknown.

So many years ago when I heard my teacher talk about it, it sounded good and true. But actually to experience it was something different. I felt frightened, hopeless, on the edge of depression, but not even able to sink into that hole.

Then one day, in the middle of my muddled mind, back in the dry and barren air of New Mexico, I realized something. That story about Siddhartha sitting under the Bodhi Tree—how he made a vow not to budge until he saw clearly into the nature of things. His determination was always touted. But, really, what was happening—all at once it seemed obvious—wasn't determination, a steeling of will that brought him home. It was a total breakdown, a collapse of everything he knew. He'd tried devout training and austerity; nothing worked. It was in his giving up—drained, exhausted, under the big, branched tree—

that with the appearance of the morning star insight exploded inside him.

For the first time I felt akin to Buddha, that skinny man in his thirties who had left his wife and child to seek the unknown. I could stop searching for some answer, some way out, some imaginary free land. Because I was so driven to find happiness, I was in the center of suffering.

But now Buddha gave me a hint of a direction. Smack in the middle of being uncomfortable, confused, restless, I could accept this groundlessness, this not knowing, as a new place, as my own country.

23

Zen at the High Chaparral

A cold, wet rain is falling; the fields are divided by barbed wire; and the slow Winnebago Creek is moving through the valley. I walk to dinner and see eight wild turkeys on the hill across from the kitchen. In 1983 we are beginning to establish a monastery on these 240 acres in the southeast corner of Minnesota, one mile from Iowa.

On weekends we go to the High Chaparral in New Albin. The owners, Herb and Ellie Mae, live in a trailer out back. Ellie Mae makes clear apple jelly, full of sugar, and as much fried chicken as you can eat on Saturday nights—with white buttered bread, coleslaw, and cottage fries. All for three dollars, and the beer is thirty-five cents. We can sit there all night if we want, slowly losing our names or where we came from, who we loved and why.

When we first went to the High Chap on Friday nights for Ellie Mae's fried cod, Greg—the head carpenter on the Zen land, whose father owned a place similar to the High Chap in Indiana and who knows everyone here—asked me if I was ready to meet some *real* Iowa farmers. When he introduced me,

they pulled him aside to ask where my people came from—
Germany? Sweden? He told them I was a Jew.

They were stunned and crinkled their noses. Then, in a mag-
nanimous gesture, they said, "Well, everyone has to come from
someplace, I guess."

Bob Stringer often sits at a corner table. Yesterday he showed
me ten dead rattlers in his car trunk. He'd smashed in their heads
near the Gibbons farm, where he found them sunning on flat
hot rocks. He pulled the biggest out of a brown paper sack. Its
fine spotted skin hung limp in his hand. He said he can collect
bounty money for them.

One noon Larry Donahue came up to the Zen land to visit us
and to give Greg some building advice. Greg was eating lunch.

Larry screwed up his face and pointed. "What the hell is that?"

"Sprouts."

"What does it taste like?"

"Here, try it." Larry put one alfalfa sprout in his mouth, and
Greg asked, "Well, what does it taste like?"

"Nothin'."

That night Larry told his wife, Marie, about the alfalfa sprouts,
and Marie asked what they tasted like.

"Nothin'."

Two days later, Larry drove up in the middle of the afternoon.
Greg came out of the kitchen to greet him, eating a rice cake
with peanut butter. Larry sat in his blue pickup, left arm hooked
over the door, and stared. "*Now* what the hell are you eating?"

"It's made of puffed rice. Wanna try it?"

"Nope." But while Larry talked about how Jim Larsen gypped
us on the price of our generator, he watched the rice cake as it
went from Greg's hand to his mouth, as he chewed and actually
swallowed it.

One morning as I was walking from town on the dirt road, Larry Donahue's father, now in his sixties, picked me up in his red Oldsmobile. Whiskey breath. His speech slurred. We wove down the road for a mile and came to a quick stop, where I got out in front of the Solberg barn, tin siding slapped over gray peeling wood. Donahue's wife had gone crazy in their big white farmhouse and killed herself ten years ago. Now Mr. Donahue wakes up early, like he did as a farmer, drives into town, and drinks until ten in the morning. I point to the fields ahead and tell him they're pretty. He looks. "I guess they are."

I realize this place isn't beautiful if you live here all of your life. It's deeper than that. The crickets fill your summer days; the hills turn brilliant in fall and white in winter. You don't make payments on your own land; you have buried your parents on it.

Duane is the best pool player in the county but says anyone from the city could beat him. He lives alone on the family farm and comes to the High Chap for company on Friday nights. The Zen students put quarters in the red flashing jukebox, and country song after country song twangs out into the dark light of the bar. We get up in our jeans and sweatshirts and work boots—I am wearing Chinese sneakers—and dance near the pool table with no apparent partner or pairing of male and female. We dance loose limbed, the way we learned in the sixties.

The three men at the bar—plus Herb, the owner, and the farmer with his pale wife and two children—watch us. The moon is almost full, and for some reason it feels extraordinary that this night we are all here together. Duane, with pool cue in hand, joins us and dances a few excited, shy steps. For moments during "Sioux City Sue," there is so much happiness that Greg kisses Duane, even though he's just lost another game to him.

I smoke a thin stogie at our long table, where David eats

french fries, then Ellie Mae's peach pie à la mode. Everyone agrees that the High Chap is sophisticated tonight, with people from all over the country—New York, California. There's even a Jew and a black person. Lots of Buddhists, a woman with a cigar, and a man kissing a man—and the people from New Albin even know our names, and we know theirs.

Outside, Ford pickups with bumper stickers are lined up in the parking lot: DON'T CUSS THE FARMER ON A FULL STOMACH. Our Toyota is parked next to them with our bumper sticker: MY KARMA RAN OVER YOUR DOGMA.

Greg, Kevin, and I drive home in the white flatbed truck the Zen center is renting. I walk to my tent. In the moonlight the Richter cornfield next door looks smoky blue, with high tassels swaying slightly in the breeze.

In a few days the new zendo will be completed. Carpenters, who spent their whole summer here without pay, are almost finished. Dana, whose family are rich grain merchants from Kansas City, tells us that if his mother calls, whatever we say, don't tell her that he's helping to build a Midwest Buddhist monastery—just tell her he's out camping for the summer.

Two carpenters from San Francisco Zen Center have come to help. The blond one repeats often: "This place has no culture! Only cows, corn, and mosquitoes!" Paul has given him the Most Miserable award—a one-inch square piece of khaki canvas. We safety-pinned it to his shirt. The material was Paul's from an earlier accident. One afternoon in June he had found three big black-and-white neighbor cows standing in the middle of his collapsed tent. Deep yellow piss formed pools in the creases. The cows mooed loudly.

Katagiri Roshi drives down from Minneapolis near the end of September. Greg shows him around. He examines everything, bending down close to have a better look at a doorknob, not saying a word, his hands clasped behind his back. The rest of us are hammering, sweeping, sanding, but breathless, waiting for Katagiri's response.

Finally he turns to Greg. "Thank you." He bows, hands in gassho.

"It's a great honor." Greg bows back.

During lunch, Roshi hears about Kevin, who has spent the last three weeks searching in an empty riverbed for perfect stones for the zendo entrance. He was stung twice by bees, almost in the same place inside his nose.

Roshi grins, exposing a mouthful of teeth, and says in English, with his Japanese precision, "Very *un-u-sual* case!"

We all laugh and slap Kevin on the back.

The next day we sit our first seven-day sesshin in the new Hokyoji zendo. On the first evening a big harvest moon hangs in the dark sky and lights a silver path to our tents.

The next night we listen to rain on the roof as we sit zazen, and then wake to a morning fog filling the valley.

By afternoon I look up to see two hawks riding the cycles of air forty feet above our heads. As I reach for a towel in the new bathhouse, I glimpse Napoleon, the ratty yellow cat we brought from the city, whom we thought we had lost, dash by through the grass.

This was the vital, wild beginning of planting Zen in the Heartland. In the beginning you can discover the secret of all that is possible to come after. But you have to pay close attention.

AFTERWORD

The Smoke of Memories

All of my life I strove to liberate the dull hours in rows of wooden desks with attached seats, the chalk dust, the unbearable long hand on the Big Ben hanging over the door, not moving fast enough. I wanted to break the tight structure of eight fifty-minute periods punctured in the middle by a cafeteria-gray lunchroom.

All of my life I wanted to communicate how light quivered at the edge of sorrow and what it was like yearning to penetrate Zen mind. I wanted enlightenment and had no idea what that was.

All of my life I have traveled, studied, taught, and searched, but it was all right here: my grandfather buttering toast in the morning, washing a glass, hanging a white sheet on the line in our suburban backyard with the mimosa out front, the soft summer breeze, the overcast sky. My grandfather once existed with his stogie cigar, Yiddish paper, strong brown calves, and fallen old chest. We all once existed—is that not amazing enough? But I had to go to Japan. I had to go to France. They were part of my existence, my time on this earth. And I am thankful for every grain of pain and every happy moment. How can I separate the good from the bad?

The Great Spring includes the Great Failure, the thoroughgoing reduction to nothing, to loss, disappointment, shame, betrayal. If we can stand still and attentive in our lives and not run away, even right in the middle of the ruins, we will find fertile ground. We will hear the sound of a songbird in a Paris chestnut tree—we may not know whether the song comes from inside us or outside. We may never have been to Paris, but it doesn't matter. We are penetrated through and through.

CREDITS

Some of the pieces in *The Great Spring* originally appeared (often in different form) in these publications:

Creative Nonfiction: "A Time of No Place" (originally titled "New Century," 2005)

Five Points: A Journal of Literature and Art: "The Lineage of Literature" (2006)

The Los Angeles Review: "Archer City" (2011)

Shambhala Sun: "Blossom" (originally titled "Blossoms Falling," 2010), "The Great Spring" (2013), "Rain and the Temple" (1999), "Losing Katherine" (2014), "Another New Year" (2012), "Meeting the Chinese in St. Paul," "A Time of No Place," "Zen at the High Chaparral" (originally titled "The Midwest Zen Summer of 1983"), "On the Shores of Lake Biwa" (2006)

Yoga Journal: "Dog-Bite Enlightenment" (1997) and "A Long Relationship with Zen" (2001)

ABOUT THE AUTHOR

NATALIE GOLDBERG is the author of fourteen books, including *Writing Down the Bones,* which has changed the way writing is taught in this country. She has led workshops and retreats for forty years nationally and internationally. She has also painted for as long as she has written. She lives in northern New Mexico. For more information, please visit www.nataliegoldberg.com.